The rise of the
schooled society

The rise of the schooled society

The history of formal schooling in England

David Wardle

Head of Education Department
Padgate College of Education

Routledge & Kegan Paul
London and Boston

First published in 1974
by Routledge & Kegan Paul Ltd
Broadway House, 68-74 Carter Lane,
London EC4V 5EL and
9 Park Street,
Boston, Mass. 02108, U.S.A.
Printed in Great Britain by
John Sherratt and Son Ltd
The St Ann's Press, Altrincham, Cheshire

ISBN 0 7100 7717 3

Library of Congress Catalog Card No. 73-86578

Contents

Acknowledgment

I wish to thank my wife for her help and encouragement at all stages in the preparation of this book, and in particular for her work upon the typescript.

Introduction

This study is not primarily a critique of the case for de-schooling. To attempt such a critique one would have to adopt a much wider approach, involving a sociological study of the existing school system, a discussion of pedagogical techniques, and perhaps most importantly, an analysis of the political and educational concepts underlying the de-schooling position. My aim is more limited: to examine the historical developments which have made it plausible to argue that formal institutional education has outgrown its usefulness and become an obstacle to social reform. Two hundred years ago such an assertion would have been patently absurd. Even a century ago it seemed obvious to social critics that the extension of formal education was among the most essential reforms to achieve; many would have placed it first. Since then there has occurred a prodigious explosion of educational provision, and when Ivan Illich writes of 'de-schooling society' we see perfectly well what he means. Whether or not one agrees with him that the growth of institutional education has gone too far, one has to admit that it has gone a very long way very quickly, and present developments indicate that, especially in higher education, it will go much further yet. Why has this situation come about? How is it related to other historical developments, political, social, economic? These are the questions to which this study is primarily directed.

Inevitably, in attempting to answer these questions I have come across material which casts some light upon the current controversy about the future, if any, of formal schooling. I have gathered the chief points together in chapter 6, where I also suggest what part a historical perspective might play in a critique of de-schooling, but it must be repeated that no effective critique can be carried through from only one point of view. One of the weaknesses of the de-schoolers' arguments I believe, is their unhistorical nature. When they attempt any explanation of the phenomenon of mass schooling, which in fact they rarely do, it amounts to no more than a crude theory of conspiracy: 'they' have invented mass schooling to preserve a hierarchy of privilege (see e.g. Reimer, 1972, pp.62-4). But, if we find this inadequate and unconvincing, we must beware of the opposite temptation of supposing that a historical examination provides all the answers. It can contribute to the discussion, perhaps particularly by puncturing over-facile causal explanations, but no more than any other discipline should it enjoy a monopoly.

Two procedural points require clarification. By the 'de-schoolers' I understand a group of writers who argue that formal institutional education has expanded too far. They are, naturally, not unanimous in their opinions, but one may abstract certain common themes: too many children are compelled to attend school for too long; the aims and achievements of schools are not subject to external validation; schools are conservative bodies, so indoctrinating their pupils that they fear radical change, or cannot even conceive of its possibility; they have usurped powers formerly held by the family, church or local community; they have an uncontrolled power of distributing life chances; education should cease to be an occupation of childhood and youth and become a life-long process. The best known of the de-schoolers in this country, I suppose, are Ivan Illich, Everett Reimer, Paul Goodman, and John Holt, and when I write of 'the de-schoolers' as a group it is to these writers that I refer.

The second point which needs some expansion is the meaning to be attached to 'school'. In a 'note for English readers' in *School is Dead* Everett Reimer mentions that in the United States the word is used to denote 'any educational institution at any level, including universities'. This is clearly the way in which Illich, Goodman and others use the term, and it is a useful convention in this controversy. Except where the context makes distinction necessary I shall use it here to avoid having to say 'schools, colleges and universities', or some clumsy generic term such as 'institutions of formal education' every time I wish to make a general statement.

Chapter 1

The changing relationship of home and school

Writers on education, whether they write from the point of view of psychology, or sociology, or teaching method, frequently find it necessary to warn readers that 'education' is not synonymous with 'schooling'. Within the last year or two this point has been urged with particular force by supporters of the de-schooling movement, who argue that 'education' may even be hampered or stultified by its association with institutions of formal instruction. As an intellectual proposition most people are prepared to accept, if they are asked to ponder the matter, that more learning takes place outside than inside schools. Indeed, it is obvious that in the first five years of life and in the lengthy period after formal education is completed, the great majority of our learning is done unconsciously, without deliberate intent, and certainly without the intervention of teacher or building.

And yet, unless our attention is specially directed to the question, we continue to see education as an activity which takes place in an institution specially set aside for the purpose, and which is given by professional teachers. In all advanced industrial societies, and in an increasing number of 'developing' countries, all children spend a substantial period in formal schooling, and, as the de-schoolers point out, there is a tendency for the length of this period to be used as an index of a society's progress. Among the most advanced nations length of schooling is being replaced as an index by the proportion of pupils who proceed to higher education—and higher education, of course, is carried on in colleges and universities, institutions of formal learning in the same class as schools.

A mental effort is needed to think away the identification of 'education' with 'schooling', but in historical terms the dominance of the school is very recent. Until the late eighteenth century formal, organized instruction of any kind was confined to a minority. Most

1

people received no education outside the home, and picked up the values and customs of their community and the skills necessary for economic survival in a more or less haphazard way. Some of these would be taught to read, and less often to write, perhaps by their mothers, but for the majority instruction, in the sense of a deliberate attempt to induce learning, was limited to casual advice, and demonstrations of skills connected with their intended trade.

For the artisan and trading classes and for their social superiors a more deliberately structured education was thought to be necessary, and this generally took the form of some kind of apprenticeship. Apprenticeship in its most precise technical sense depended upon the control of industry by guilds and similar societies, and it dominated the educational scene from at least the fourteenth to the mid-eighteenth centuries. Numerous charities existed for the purpose of apprenticing poor children, and many charity schools set aside funds to meet the premiums of old boys and girls. In the late eighteenth century the political and economic climate became unfavourable to guilds, which inhibited technical innovation and the mobility of labour, and were relics of a society in which competition was looked upon as a vice rather than as one of the mainsprings of economic progress. As they declined so did apprenticeship, which retained its importance as a means of vocational training only in certain of the professions—law and surgery for example—until it was revived in the twentieth century. But the custom of sending children into other households for their education extended beyond those families which bound their children to formal apprenticeship. Among the nobility and gentry boys were placed wherever possible in houses of men of superior rank, the king's household being the training ground of large numbers of youths of particularly aristocratic birth. One of the duties of a nobleman was to provide an education for the sons of those gentlemen who were considered to fall within his allegiance, and service with a man distinguished in war or politics was an important recommendation for an aspiring young man. According to an Italian visitor to England in about 1500, this custom was peculiarly English, at least in its universal application (Williams, 1967, p.196):

The want of affection in the English is strongly manifested towards their children, for having kept them at home till they arrive at the age of seven or nine years at the utmost, they put them out, both males and females, to hard service in the houses of other people, binding them generally for another seven or more years. And these are called apprentices, and during that time they perform all the most menial offices; and few are born who are exempted from this fate, for everyone, however rich he may be, sends away his children into the house of others whilst he, in return, receives those of strangers into his own.

This aristocratic form of apprenticeship seems to have died out earlier than the industrial form, and to have been in decline in the seventeenth century, although by no means extinct when Locke was writing. He was still able to recommend the nobleman's family as an educational agency on the grounds that the household was a public place, providing an initiation into the business of government and administration, and experience of the adult world. But by his time the membership and function even of the aristocratic family were becoming increasingly restricted. A distinction was being drawn between the 'family' and the 'household', and the division between family and servants was widening socially, functionally, and even geographically as private apartments were separated from servants' quarters and business premises. It was no longer socially acceptable for a young nobleman to serve part of his training in a menial capacity, and to take a revealing example, the word 'valet' lost its meaning of a young boy attending upon a lord, and gained its modern meaning of a professional 'gentleman's gentleman'. When Rousseau wrote in the middle of the eighteenth century, he agreed with Locke in recommending education at home, but for precisely the opposite reason—that the child at home was protected from the adult world, and so preserved in his innocence.

Undoubtedly the replacement of the medieval extended household by the modern nuclear family contributed to the decline of apprenticeship in both its aristocratic and its industrial forms, but its significance for us is wider than this. The 'household' was inescapably an institution committed, among other functions, to formal education. The instruction given to pages and apprentices was, in theory at least, deliberate and continuous, and extended into the moral as well as the more strictly vocational field. No doubt in practice this instruction was frequently neglected, but the theoretical responsibilities of the household for the education of its members was well enough understood. But when, particularly in the eighteenth century, the family drew in upon itself it cast off its function as an agent of formal education, while retaining, and indeed emphasizing its affective aspects. Here already is one important reason for the rise of schooling. When mass elementary education was first mooted at the turn of the eighteenth and nineteenth centuries, its advocates were faced by an educational vacuum. Formal apprenticeship was dying, and was often merely a polite euphemism for child exploitation, while the family either accepted no educational responsibility or wished to delegate its educational function. The school was a necessary expedient to fill the gap.

Of course the school was not a new institution in the eighteenth century; schools had a recognized, although subordinate, place in the educational scheme. They were thought to have four functions. Of these the most extensive was teaching the rudiments to children preparing to enter apprenticeship. This is the branch of schooling which has left the fewest traces because it was usually undertaken in small private schools which have left no permanent records and were frequently relatively short-lived; but such private schools were very numerous and were enormously varied in their social and academic pretensions. At one end of the scale were cheap 'common day' schools offering no more than reading, with perhaps writing and arithmetic for a few long-staying pupils. Children left these schools very young—certainly by eight or nine years—and entered unskilled or semi-skilled trades, and an important part of the schools' business was child minding for working mothers. Far removed from these were 'writing schools' which prepared pupils for apprenticeship to highly skilled crafts and for posts in offices, warehouses and so on. Such pupils were unlikely to be indentured before they were twelve or fourteen years old, and had to obtain a good level of literacy and numerical competence. As the name of these schools suggest, many of them attempted to teach rather more than the rudiments, and offered directly vocational courses in commercial writing, shorthand, commercial arithmetic, book-keeping, and occasionally in less common occupations such as surveying or pharmacy. This constituted virtually the only available technical training outside apprenticeship.

A far smaller number of schools offered a definitely academic course, intended for the education of a small intelligentsia, and particularly for intending clergymen. The grammar schools had been established for this purpose and dominated the field until the eighteenth century, when many of them went into decline, their clientele chiefly being absorbed by superior private schools of the class usually called 'academies', although a few grammar schools elevated themselves to the status of national institutions forming the nucleus of the present public schools. The work of these schools was intended to be preliminary to university, although for most schools very few pupils did in fact proceed to Oxford or Cambridge, and was almost universally limited to the classics—thus, incidentally, presupposing the existence of 'petty schools' to supply them with pupils ready to embark on Latin. From their foundation they were attended not only by boys preparing for the Church, but also by middle class children who might or might not be intended for university, but who certainly had no clerical ambitions. By the sixteenth century, and perhaps earlier, the beginnings were visible of the notion that one way of indicating the status of one's family was to give one's children a lengthy schooling proving presumably that one could do without the profit to be gained from putting them out to work.

But even in the field of strictly academic education schools did not by any means enjoy a monopoly, for even after parents had ceased to send their children to other households for instruction, they inclined to keep them at home to be educated by tutors or governesses rather than to send them out to school. The wealthiest families employed resident tutors for the elder children who were to be initiated into the classics—John Locke served in this capacity for a time—while the preparatory education of younger children and of the girls of the house was supervised by governesses, who might be assisted in specific subjects by visiting tutors. Fathers with more modest incomes hired visiting tutors, often private school proprietors who regularly supplemented their income in this way. If anything, education at home became more widespread in the eighteenth century. Contemporary writers on education were generally opposed to schooling. Locke and Rousseau, as we have already noted, agreed on this point even if they arrived at the same conclusion from very different premises, and their views were confirmed by, among others, Joseph Priestley and R. L. Edgeworth. David Williams in his *Treatise on Education* of 1774 extended a grudging tolerance to schools, but only as a temporary expedient, until men would be 'capable of presiding over their own families, and educating their children: and render schools themselves unnecessary'. It is not absolutely clear how far the popularity of home education with educational theorists reflected a genuine increase in the number of parents who supervised their children's studies, but the condition of public and grammar schools in the eighteenth century gave much ammunition to their critics. The classic curriculum was archaic and taught in an unimaginative way involving much rote learning and the use of corporal punishment. Relations between teachers and pupils were generally hostile and not infrequently broke out into open revolt, while teachers exercised little influence over pupils outside the classroom, so that bullying and immorality were rife. Thoughtful parents might well have hesitated to send their children to such institutions, which, in any event, provided very few places indeed for girls.

There was one other function which was thought proper for schools—the provision of education for those children who, through the absence or incompetence of parents, were in need of upbringing outside the home. Orphans were the obvious subjects for such education, and charity schools were particularly concerned to provide for them, sometimes offering clothing and eventual apprenticeship as well as the basic schooling. But it was also recognized that it might be necessary to assist poor families, not only because of the financial burden involved in bringing up children, but also because parents were too ignorant or feckless to sustain their responsibilities. Until the end of the eighteenth century it was supposed that the number of children requiring charitable assistance in this way was relatively limited and, indeed, there was a common feeling that the acceptance of charity was a disgrace to be avoided wherever possible by respectable working men. But the definition of parental incompetence was clearly a matter which allowed for considerable elasticity, and there was no logical reason why education under this rubric might not be extended to a far larger proportion of the population if changing circumstances seemed to make this necessary.

In the nineteenth and twentieth centuries formal schooling took a progressively more important role in education, until by degrees it assumed the dominant position which it holds today. This development occurred in three dimensions, which are distinguished here for purposes of analysis, although they overlapped chronologically and were closely related causally. First, schooling was extended to cover the whole population and not simply the groups mentioned in the previous section. Second, the length of school life was increased. Third, the sphere of operations of the school was widened to include various activities and services outside the traditional understanding of its role—medical treatment, meals, organized games, careers advice, etc. Very recently the same process of expansion has begun in the higher education field, and the same three dimensions have been apparent—a larger proportion of the population has entered higher education, students have stayed for longer, and non-academic activities have increased in importance. In this chapter the process of development will simply be described, explanation and comment being left for later discussion.

In tracing the expansion of the school system to include the whole population, two distinct processes have to be examined—the extension down the social scale to classes not previously considered to require formal schooling; and the substitution, within the upper and middle classes, of schooling in place of domestic education by parents, tutors and governesses.

In the first case, the beginning of the change can be dated with some accuracy to the last few years of the eighteenth century. Schools for the poor were not, of course, a new venture. They were fairly numerous in the seventeenth century, when they formed a frequent subject for endowment, and early in the eighteenth century the Society for Promoting Christian Knowledge inspired an extensive and successful campaign for the establishment of charity schools. But these schools differed from nineteenth-century foundations in that their efforts were intensive rather than extensive. They were generally fairly small—twenty to thirty pupils being a fair average—and their enrolment was frequently limited by their foundation deeds to a fixed number of pupils. On the other hand they aimed to keep their children for a substantial length of time and to achieve a relatively advanced level of learning; some of them found no difficulty in converting themselves into respectable secondary schools as the initial wave of enthusiasm for social rescue work died away. Clothing, often a distinctive uniform, was provided by some schools, and funds for apprenticing old scholars or setting up girls in domestic service were not unusual. In contrast, the Sunday schools and elementary day schools which appeared at the turn of the eighteenth and nineteenth centuries aimed to give a rudimentary education to as large a number of children as the funds would allow, the reduction of per capita expenditure being a prime consideration with teachers and managers. Both Lancaster and Bell made a particular virtue of the ability of one teacher assisted by monitors to control huge classes, Lancaster speaking with approval of schools of five hundred pupils. Few schools in the early nineteenth century were, in fact, as large as this, but in large towns, schools of between two and three hundred were not at all unusual, and at the census of 1851 the average size of voluntary elementary schools was ninety-one pupils, a figure which would be affected by the large number of very small village schools. The curriculum of these schools was extremely restricted. Sunday schools were naturally unable to attempt any very ambitious academic performances because of the short time for which their children were present, and religious instruction and reading formed their basic syllabus. Some Sunday schools ran evening classes at which writing was taught, and even in a very few cases very elementary arithmetic, but secular instruction was prohibited in many schools with the exception of reading, a necessary preparation for study of the Bible. Day schools could attempt rather more, but the short school life, large numbers of pupils, and the low quality of the teachers prevented much progress. Even in 1851 while all day schools taught reading, 90 per cent of public elementary schools and only 55 per cent of private schools taught writing, and 84 per cent of public schools and 48 per cent of private schools taught arithmetic. No doubt some of the supporters of Sunday schools and elementary day schools would have liked to offer more advanced work, but they were quite conscious that with the limited funds available to them they must choose between an intensive education for a few, and a rudimentary education for many, and they decided upon the latter. Advertisements for elementary schools sometimes made this point quite explicitly by stating that beneficiaries from the charity could expect no other assistance than schooling. Presumably some parents, with the example of the old charity schools in front of them, hoped for their children to be clothed or to receive other similar benefits.

The expansion of school provision achieved in this period was remarkable. An enquiry conducted in 1786 reported that there were then 4,100 endowed schools for the children of the poor with 165,000 pupils and 14,300 unendowed schools with 478,000 pupils (see Jones, 1964, p.322). By 1833 there were 38,971 day schools catering for 1,275,000 pupils, while, in addition there were 16,828 Sunday schools with 1,550,000 pupils (see Smith, 1931, p.220). Social statistics in the early nineteenth century were extremely unreliable, and it will not do to place detailed reliance on these figures, but the general picture is plain enough, and the expansion was cumulative, the most rapid increase in day school accommodation taking place between 1818 and 1833, when the number of schools and of scholars effectively doubled. This represents a massive and extremely well sustained charitable effort, suggesting that the classes sufficiently well off to contribute to such movements regarded the establishment of public elementary education as a matter of real importance. Many of the day schools were private-venture profit-making establishments; in 1786 certainly the great majority of the non-endowed schools fell into this category. But an increasing proportion were provided by charity. In 1851 over 15,400 public elementary schools were recorded by the educational census—the first really reliable set of national statistics on education. The number of schools was maintained throughout the century, and in 1900 there were still about 15,000 voluntary elementary schools with two million pupils.

But in the meantime public concern about schooling had shown itself in a new form. In the eighteenth century education was conceived to be a private matter. Whether a child was educated at home, or sent to school, or whether his education was totally neglected was taken to be a question affecting himself and his parents alone, and it was no-one else's right or duty to interfere. As we have seen, this rule was relaxed in the case of children whose parents were demonstrably unwilling or unable to meet their obligations, but even then assistance was given as an act of private charity. It was not supposed either that there was any necessity for all children to be formally educated, or that any public authority had a duty to provide education. The Church of England had more or less given up its claim, sporadically enforced in the seventeenth century, to supervise and license schools and teachers, and state provision of education was hardly even an academic question. In fact, any notion of a *system* of education was scouted, even the Society for Promoting Christian Knowledge conscientiously avoiding the role of educational legislator and confining itself to the encouragement of local enterprise. (The reasons behind this attitude are discussed in chapter 5.) In both respects the nineteenth-century advocates of elementary education took up very different positions. The aim of Sunday schools and monitorial schools was to bring into the educational fold all those children whose parents were unable to afford an efficient education, and statisticians were much exercised to determine what proportion of the population ought to be in school at any given moment, and how near the country was to achieving this proportion. Frequent comparisons were made with other countries— France, Prussia, the Netherlands and Switzerland were often referred to—the usual conclusion being that, while progress was certainly being made, it was by no means rapid enough.

An important feature of these international comparisons was that some of the European countries, in theory at least, had state educational systems with compulsory school attendance. Few people in England were yet prepared for a national system of education in the twentieth-century sense, but the question of government support for private effort was reopened, and in 1833 the first grant was made to assist with the building of schoolhouses. At first the grant was extremely small and limited in scope, but a precedent had been established and within a few years further grants were being made for teacher training, to supplement teachers' salaries etc., and by degrees the government was drawn into the management as well as the building of schools. From £20,000 in 1833 the annual grant rose to £150,000 in 1851, after which the increase accelerated rapidly, so that by 1859 the grant was £837,000. Up to this point the extension of government influence had occurred more through inertia than through deliberate policy, but during the 1850s and 1860s the relationship of the state to education was vigorously discussed, and a number of abortive bills were put before Parliament. Eventually Forster's Act was passed in 1870. Two provisions of this Act are of special importance here. In districts where a shortage of school accommodation existed, schools boards could be elected which could use rate aid for building and maintaining schools. And these school boards were allowed to produce by-laws making school attendance compulsory.

From this point progress was rapid. Many school boards used their powers of compulsion, and by a series of Acts between 1876 and 1893 the whole country was covered by school boards and school attendance committees, which served the same purpose, and school attendance was made compulsory to the age of eleven years. The principle was now established that all children should receive a certain minimum period of formal education, whilst it was assumed virtually without question that education, to come within the meaning of the Acts, must take place in school. From the 1870s to the present day the minimum legal period of schooling has been progressively extended, a development which will be described later in the chapter.

While the incidence of schooling was being widened to include the poorer members of the working class, a similar expansion was taking place in the more socially exalted branch of education which dealt with children of the upper and middle classes. The assumption is still sometimes made that in the seventeenth and eighteenth century the public schools and grammar schools enjoyed the same dominant position in secondary education which they have held for the past seventy years; but this is not so. Dr Hans has investigated the education of some 3,500 eighteenth-century notables who appear in the *Dictionary of National Biography*, and his results are summarized as follows (Hans, 1951, p.19):

From 9 public schools	780
20 selected grammar schools	209
150 other grammar schools	385
English Dissenting Academies	212
Catholic colleges	125
Private academies and schools	314
Scottish/Irish/Welsh schools	414
Private tutors and home	967

It will be noticed that rather over a quarter of all these cases were educated entirely at home, more than came from any single category of school, and, in fact, these figures rather underestimate the importance of domestic education since very many children who later attended public schools or private academies received their preparatory education at home. Only the major public schools approached the popularity of home teaching, and, while they held their position in spite of being subjected to very severe criticism in the late eighteenth and early nineteenth centuries, the grammar schools certainly declined in educational importance during this period.

The first sign of change was the popularity of private schools in the last quarter of the eighteenth century. The period from 1770 to 1830 was the age of prosperity for the 'classical academy'. These schools were usually very small, providing for six to twelve boarders, and they were generally run by clergymen, often in their own vicarages. They were expensive, charging fees of upwards of sixty guineas per year with extensive extras, and their curriculum was based on the classics, although some offered wider courses including mathematics and science. Advertisements made a particular point of the small number of scholars, the close supervision of the proprietor, and the family atmosphere, and it is obvious that the proprietors were aiming to attract parents who objected to the neglect and low moral tone of the public schools, but who either could not afford private tuition, or wished for their boys to enjoy a carefully controlled companionship with others of their own age. Many of these schools were in fairly remote places, and the wide placing of their advertisements suggest that they hoped for a national clientele.

Considerably cheaper than these exclusive establishments were the 'English and Commercial Academies' which also enjoyed great prosperity at this time. They were relatively large, often employing several assistant teachers, and were generally to be found in towns, since, although most of them took a few boarders, the bulk of their business was done with local children who attended daily. The social class which they served was rather below that of the 'classical academies'. Although they liked to advertise their classical courses, their proprietors were well aware that most of their pupils would leave in their early teens and take up relatively humble occupations as farmers, shop-keepers, clerks, apothecaries etc. and so they were not above offering courses with an explicitly vocational bias. While the 'classical academy' was looking for its custom among parents who might be thinking of sending boys to public schools, the 'English and Commercial Academy' was operating in the vacuum left by the decline of grammar schools, but in both cases the number and success of these schools suggest that they were in a rapidly expanding market. In Nottingham about 1800, for a town of nearly 30,000 inhabitants, there were, apart from three endowed schools, five private schools which enjoyed a particular prestige and some twenty other schools offering their services in the same field. In addition, numerous schools from out of town found it worthwhile to advertise in the local papers, some from as far away as Wetherby and Manchester.

In the early nineteenth century, if a group of people wished to achieve a mutually advantageous object, they generally formed an 'association' for the purpose. In the absence of the welfare state of today these 'associations' were immensely numerous and widespread in their activities. The recognized way of obtaining the arrest of criminals, the return of stolen property and the prevention of further offences was through membership of associations which offered rewards which, it was hoped, would tempt accomplices and receivers of stolen goods. Working people formed friendly societies to ensure various benefits including, very often, insurance against the disgrace of a pauper's funeral. The National Society and the British and Foreign School Society were classical cases of associations on the very largest scale, while hospitals, asylums, dispensaries and similar charities were established in most large towns at this period as a result of more local efforts. As the demand for what would now be termed secondary education increased, and the inability of existing endowed schools to meet the demand became progressively more obvious, it was natural that the idea should be taken up of promoting associations to provide secondary schools. Some private schools were very good indeed, but in an expanding market, and with no system whatsoever of quality control, it was only to be expected that the quality varied widely, and that parents were frequently dissatisfied. Furthermore, the best schools tended to be very expensive, and much of the new demand for secondary education was coming from business and professional men who found sixty to one hundred guineas per year per child a serious drain on their resources. These men were often conscious that they occupied a social position between the two classes for whom education had traditionally been provided—the nobility and gentry with public schools, and the working class with charity schools—and that they were out of place in either milieu. They were looking for a category of school which catered specifically for their social class. Professor Simon quotes a Leicester clergyman who puts the case quite precisely, when referring to the foundation of Leicester Collegiate School in 1836 (1960, p.116):

> These [sc. public] schools are more particularly the resort of the young members of the noblest and wealthiest families . . . . But we of the middle class must strive to hold our own, we will labour to hold our proportionate rank—to support our middle station, and if possible to elevate that station. This school will doubtless have that powerful tendency.

Nathaniel Woodard, writing a few years later, expressed the same sentiments rather more bluntly (Heeney, 1969, p.10): 'The upper classes have taken care of themselves and the lower classes have been well cared for; but between these two fruitful regions lies a vast tract of howling wilderness and imposture'.

The first 'proprietorial' schools, which was the generic name applied to these establishments at the time, were founded in the 1820s and 1830s. Most of the schools founded at this time were day schools catering for middle class children of the larger towns; Liverpool and Leicester each had two foundations. They were designed to fill very much the same position as the old grammar schools, but with curricula better designed for nineteenth-century conditions, and without the atmosphere of gentlemanly incompetence which hung over so many contemporary grammar schools due, in part at least, to the dead hand of archaic foundation statutes. But, although this movement was not entirely unsuccessful, secondary education in public day schools was not to make a major recovery until the last quarter of the century. Of more immediate importance was the revival of the public schools. This is generally attributed chiefly to the work of Thomas Arnold at Rugby between 1828 and 1842, and, although other schools and other headmasters made important contributions, it is at all events true that the public schools made a remarkable recovery in efficiency and public estimation in this period. One of the attractions of the public schools to the mid-nineteenth-century parent seems to have been the boarding principle, and when the second wave of proprietorial schools was founded in the 1860s many of them were boarding schools, and have since been accepted as public schools themselves, for example Wellington 1859, Clifton 1860, Malvern 1862, Radley 1863 and Haileybury 1864. By no means all the proprietorial schools were as successful as these. Several failed altogether, and others reverted to private schools. The besetting problem, of course, was the difficulty of sustaining the interest of subscribers.

The 1860s were as critical for the expansion of secondary education as they were for elementary education, and to complete the parallel it was at this time that the government took a hand in the situation, an indication of the degree to which public concern had been stirred up. The Clarendon Commission investigated the public schools, while the Taunton Commission examined the rest of the field. The condition of endowed schools, particularly grammar schools, had been a scandal for many years, and the facts about individual schools were made public from time to time. For example in 1818 it emerged that the headmaster of Pocklington School, enjoying a stipend in excess of £600, had not attended for over a year, while the assistant, with £300, was deaf, and the pupils were sent to other schools. But the enquiry commissions accumulated a quantity of evidence of apathy, incompetence and downright fraud which was difficult to ignore. A commission was appointed to supervise the reorganization of educational endowments. It worked with a politically inconvenient ardour and after a few years was merged with the Charity Commission, but the work of rationalization continued, if at a reduced rate, and valuable progress was made in freeing schools from cramping regulations, re-allocating funds earmarked for obsolete purposes, and in particular in making endowments available for the education of girls, for whom the provision of public secondary schooling had been grossly inadequate.

The rise in the demand for secondary education accelerated rapidly in the last quarter of the nineteenth century. This was due in large part to a widening of the definition of secondary education, and thus of the proportion of the population thought to be potential pupils. Up to this time it had been supposed that secondary schools would cater for boys of the upper and middle classes. The lower boundary was not fixed with any certainty, but no-one doubted that social class was a critical measure of suitability for secondary education. Equally there was little doubt that academic or vocational education at this level was a male activity. A few girls' schools offered a genuinely rigorous curriculum, but they were rare, and the education of most girls was diffuse and trivial, comprising chiefly 'the accomplishments'—water colour painting, music, deportment, perhaps a foreign language. Nothing was studied in any depth, and professional competence in any activity was regarded as unladylike.

In the 1880s a demand arose that opportunities for secondary education be extended down the social scale. In part this was a demand from potential consumers. Many of the larger school boards found themselves faced by numbers of pupils who wished to remain at school—or whose parents wished them to remain—after they had passed through all the standards. These were generally the more able pupils, and their parents hoped for them to receive an education which would improve their sale value on the employment market. Something more ambitious was wanted than mere repetition of normal elementary school work, but elementary schools were perpetually understaffed and their teachers as a rule lacked the knowledge or experience to teach anything much beyond the rudiments. The natural response was to establish central schools to which these advanced pupils could be drafted, staffing them with relatively well qualified teachers. In this way several school boards, chiefly those in the large towns, founded higher grade schools, which, as they got into their stride, progressively approximated to secondary schools, offering courses leading to school leaving examinations, and frequently experimenting with vocationally biased courses.

Higher grade schools were expensive to run, and secondary education for the working class was such an innovation that one might have expected them to have encountered determined opposition. Indeed, their success did arouse some concern among teachers and others who feared that the academic and social standards of secondary education were endangered. But the extension of the social catchment area of secondary education was strongly supported from two very different quarters. Working class political leaders joined with socialists in advocating it from one point of view, while nationalists and imperialists were associated with industrialists in offering support for quite different reasons. By the early 1900s, although the higher grade schools themselves were dismantled, a consensus had been reached that secondary education, however that might be defined, should be open to working class children who displayed unusual talents. In 1907 by the Free Place regulations a system was established by which elementary school children could be transferred to grammar schools upon the results of an examination. A substantial government grant, by the standards of the day, was paid to schools which participated in the scheme.

Contemporary with the call for secondary education to be extended to selected members of the working class was a demand that girls be offered a more solid education. Between 1869 and 1897 the Charity Commission raised the number of endowed girls' schools from fourteen to eighty-six, and converted thirty-one boys' schools into mixed schools, while it was a feature of the higher grade schools that many of them provided for girls as well as for boys. The Girls' Public Day School Trust was founded in 1872 to set up schools for girls of a rather superior social class to the higher grade schools, and much of the power behind the agitation for university extension came from the movement for women's education. The combined effect of the extension of secondary education to women and to children of the working class was greatly to increase the demand for school accommodation, while at the same time forcing a major reconsideration of the role of secondary education, both in the life of the individual and as a national investment. The grammar schools, moribund for so long, now recovered and new schools were added, particularly after 1902 when local education authorities were given responsibility for secondary as well as for elementary education. Together with the higher grade schools and the senior departments of elementary schools, in which standards of work rose sharply in this period, they squeezed out the private schools, which now became very expensive luxuries rarely able to rival the equipment and teaching power of rate and tax assisted schools. By 1902 it was firmly established that secondary education would be received in schools, and that for the great majority these schools would be within the state system. Events of the past seventy years have served to reinforce this conclusion.

In the nineteenth century the school population increased chiefly because schooling was extended to cover an ever wider sector of the nation. By the end of the century everyone, with negligible exceptions, spent some period of their life in school, and a new factor began to operate, accelerating the increase in school attendance. This was a progressive lengthening of school life. It is difficult to suggest any useful average figure for school life in the early nineteenth century, partly because evidence is rather scarce, and partly because of the very large fluctuations from class to class and district to district. Many, perhaps the majority, never attended school at all for any significant length of time, any schooling which they received being limited to spasmodic appearances at Sunday school or dame school. Even those working class children who attended National or British schools did so for an extremely short time, and this was frequently interrupted by lengthy absences if opportunities were offered of profitable employment. In the 1840s HMIs and head teachers were in general agreement that such children might achieve a school life of rather under two years, perhaps spread over three to five years, and certainly completed by the time they were ten years old. A turnover of pupils of 100 per cent in one year was not at all unusual for elementary schools. These schools were better organized than cheap private schools and brought greater pressure to bear on parents and pupils to secure attendance, so that it is reasonably certain that their results were at least as good as anyones else's in the field. Very little progress was made before 1870, increased efforts by teachers and managers being cancelled out by the fact that they were drawing pupils from classes which were more than ever reluctant to insist upon their children's attendance. Even in 1870 the average school life in inspected elementary schools—by and large the most efficient of their type—was only 2·55 years, and it remained generally true that schools were used as child-minding institutions by working mothers. When the school boards investigated their problems on assuming office, they usually found that elementary schools had plenty of vacancies and that a normal average attendance was about two-thirds of those children whose names appeared on the roll.

Middle class children, as was only to be expected, attended school for longer, but even for them school life was short by modern standards. Boys who were not proceeding to university, and only a tiny minority did so, were expected to leave even the more prosperous academies at twelve to fourteen years to enter offices or take up apprenticeships. The surviving records of one private school show that of twenty-eight boarders who entered in 1809 (Wardle, 1971, p.154):

> 5 stayed less than 1 year
> 12 stayed 1 year and less than 2
> 5 stayed 2 years and less than 3
> 1 stayed 3 years and less than 4
> 4 stayed 4 years and less than 5
> 1 stayed 5 years.

This school offered a four-year course, but, although it was regarded as one of the half-dozen best academies in the town, fewer than a quarter of its pupils remained for so long.

For working class children the leaving age rose very sharply when compulsory attendance was established. In 1897 the average school life in inspected elementary schools was 7·05 years, and by that time this figure was more significant as an average since the great majority of elementary schools were inspected. Middle class children were not affected particularly by the introduction of compulsion since they had always attended school until about twelve years, and for them major change was long delayed. The appearance of public leaving examinations tended to raise the leaving age to fifteen or sixteen years, but many did not stay to sit these examinations, and very few stayed on after the equivalent of 'O' level. As late as 1937 only 15 per cent of pupils in grant-aided secondary schools remained for six years, and this represented a mere 4 per cent of the age group. The Robbins Report of 1963 includes figures which demonstrate the course of the rise in the school leaving age (see Table 1):

Table I *Percentage of children at various ages in full-time education*

Age	1870	1902	1938	1962
10 years	40	100	100	100
14 years	2	9	38	100
17 years	1	2	4	15
19 years	1	1	2	7

Although education has been a growth industry since at least the early nineteenth century, this growth has accelerated remarkably since the Second World War. The school leaving age has been raised to fifteen years, and is now, after long delays, to be raised to sixteen, but the legal minimum age for leaving is becoming decreasingly relevant as a measure of school life. Between 1950 and 1966, while the total school population rose by 24 per cent, the number of pupils aged fifteen years and over in full-time schooling increased from 290,000 to 782,000, and in the same period the proportion of the age group remaining in school after seventeen years almost exactly doubled. Correspondingly massive increases were recorded in the number of candidates for public examinations. Passes in individual subjects at 'O' level multiplied nearly three times, and at 'A' level the expansion was faster still. In addition, the new Certificate of Secondary Education attracted a large entry, chiefly from a class of pupils who would not previously have sat for leaving examinations. This is striking evidence of the way in which formal education has succeeded in selling itself as a desirable, indeed a necessary, commodity. Complaints are still heard of pupils' dislike of school and of their rejection of its values. No doubt these complaints have some validity, even if the situation to which they refer is not so novel as some commentators appear to believe, but the hard fact remains that a large and progressively increasing proportion of the school population is choosing to remain at school after the minimum leaving age, forcing upon teachers and administrators a radical reappraisal of the personal and social function of secondary education. This is a paradigm case of the type of development which we have to explain in this study.

A similar explosive growth has affected higher education. Until the Second World War this was very much a minority concern; in 1902 only 1·2 per cent of the relevant age group were in full time higher education. The proportion rose to 2·7 per cent by 1924 and then was stable until 1939. After the war there was fairly rapid expansion until the early 1960s when it accelerated enormously. The number of undergraduate students at university increased two-and-a-half times between 1953 and 1967, the increase in postgraduate students being more rapid still. In addition, a whole new area of higher education grew up outside the university system, with polytechnics offering degree and higher degree courses in a way which really had no parallel at all in the pre-war educational system. Even colleges of education, very much the poor relations of the higher education world, enjoyed a period of expansion in the middle 1960s when enrolment increased and standards of work rose to include preparation for first degrees.

So far it has been taken for granted that one lengthens school life by raising the leaving age, but an obvious alternative is to lower the age of admission. One effect of the introduction of compulsion was to produce a standard age for commencing school, which has always been taken, in this country, to be five years of age. Before this time elementary schools had regularly taken children much younger than this and, indeed, when board schools first began to be overcrowded it was the infant departments which felt the pressure, because they still retained many under-age children, No doubt, in the minds of parents at least, their chief function remained that of baby minding. Only later, particularly in the 1880s, did the overcrowding move into the upper standards, producing the demand for quasi-secondary education which was discussed earlier in the chapter. The call for institutions to cater for pre-school children has never entirely disappeared, and in time of war when married women's work was of national importance, efforts were made to increase provision in this area. Quite recently however, this call has become much more insistent. Associations have been formed to encourage local voluntary action and to campaign for official support, and numerous playgroups and nurseries have been established on a basis of mutual self-help. In some respects this is a peculiarly interesting development, for the pressure for expansion seems to have arisen quite spontaneously from parents who have persisted in agitation in the face of inertia, not to say hostility, from central and local authorities. As yet, the proportion of the age group for whom playgroups are available is fairly small, but it is of considerable consequence in the context of this enquiry that there should be an increasing demand for educational institutions which is so very clearly not a product of official propaganda, and which is making ground to all appearances against the wishes of powerful vested educational interests. In discussing the dominance of schooling in the modern educational scene, this phenomenon is critical in a way very similar to the expansion of demand at the other end of school life.

We have considered educational expansion in two dimensions—the extension of schooling to new classes of the population, and the lengthening of school life. Now it is time to adopt a third viewpoint, and look at the way in which the terms of reference of the school and of the educational system in general have been widened to include functions which previously belonged to the individual or to the family, or were not really felt to be necessary at all. It is possible to exaggerate the academic bias of nineteenth-century schools, and it is one of the aims of this study to suggest that the reasons for extending and institutionalizing education in the nineteenth century were rather complex, with the conveying of information, even of a technical character, coming quite low on most educators' lists of priorities. But it remains true that schools today have a more complicated and diffuse role than ever before, and that they have more varied contacts with the surrounding community.

A critical period in this change was the turn of the nineteenth and twentieth centuries. The curriculum of the elementary school widened in the 1880s and 1890s very largely because the longer school life and greater regularity of attendance gave schools the opportunity to attempt more ambitious schemes of work. But on the whole, what was happening here was that schools were really succeeding in teaching syllabuses which had previously existed only as aspirations. More interesting to us is the inclusion of activities which had not so far appeared even on paper syllabuses and which, in many cases, only came to be considered as within the sphere of influence of schools in this period. Physical education was not entirely a newcomer. Fashionable private schools had made rather a point of physical activities a hundred years previously, very probably under the influence of Rousseau or Locke or their various interpreters, and swimming baths and gymnastic apparatus were fairly common in such institutions. In the second half of the nineteenth century the public schools moved towards the cult of physical activity which has since come to be considered as one of their distinguishing features. Even in elementary schools experiments had been tried with organized games, chiefly football and athletics, some of the larger and bolder school boards organizing leagues and competitions. Swimming was popular in towns well supplied with public baths. But these were all strictly extra-curricular; it was in the 1890s and early 1900s that physical education was established as a basic part of the curriculum. The code of 1890 allowed time spent in 'suitable physical exercises' to be counted towards attendance, and five years later a grant was paid in respect of physical education. In 1906 a further relaxation of the regulations permitted organized games to be included in attendance. The Board of Education even drew up a course of drill, originally on military lines, but later rewritten under the influence of the currently popular Swedish drill. The significance to us of these official developments is twofold. They provide evidence that the physical welfare of children was exciting so much concern in influential quarters that the government was prepared to countenance public expenditure. And they illustrate the way in which an appeal to the school as an agent of social policy was becoming a natural response for publicists, politicians and administrators.

This concern for physical welfare was characteristic of the period and produced other important educational innovations. School dinners had been provided by charitable effort in some schools since the early ragged schools of the 1840s and more extensive schemes were produced by school boards, chiefly in urban areas where the problems of poverty were most conspicuous. But no public money was available so that such schemes were generally ephemeral and inevitably affected relatively few children. An Act of 1906 enabled local education authorities to subsidize meals with the proceeds of a $\frac{1}{2}$d rate. It was a permissive measure and many authorities did not take advantage of it, those that did so often making unsatisfactory arrangements with sub-contractors. Nevertheless, the possibility existed of an effective school meal service, and the failure of individual schemes does not affect the fact that schools were being asked to undertake another venture into welfare. The same is true of the introduction of the school medical service in the following year, again on a permissive basis. At first it was concerned only with inspection, and treatment could not be provided until 1914, inspection and treatment being made a statutory duty in 1921.

Closely related to these developments was the treatment of handicapped children. Here again, what happened was that official blessing was given to pioneer efforts by school boards and voluntary bodies and, what was perhaps of more immediate importance, public funds were made chargeable for special schools and classes. Blind and deaf children had received some attention even before the school board period; the first school for the blind seems to have been founded in Liverpool in 1791, and several others were opened before 1800. Various school boards established special schools for the blind and deaf, often receiving grants on them as if they were infant schools under gentlemen's agreements with HMIs, because the pupils were, of course, unable to meet the standard requirements of the elementary school code. Some even set up special classes for children with other physical and mental handicaps, often run on kindergarten lines. But no special grants could be claimed for these schools, which were very expensive in terms of staff and equipment, until the Defective and Epileptic Children's Act was passed in 1899. This again was permissive, and local education authorities were not obliged to adopt it until 1914, some categories of handicapped children remaining outside the scope of legislation until 1918.

There was public concern about the moral as well as the physical welfare of children and young people, and especially about the children who, leaving school as early as possible, entered employment at an age when they were still in need of adult guidance. Efforts to provide education and organized recreation for this group were repeatedly made in the period between 1890 and 1914, by school boards and local education authorities, and by voluntary agencies of all kinds. The Boys' Brigade was formed in 1883 and had 50,000 members by 1900. It was copied in many of its aspects by the Boys' Life Brigade of 1889 and the Church Lads' Brigade of 1891. In the early years of the twentieth century the Scout and Guide movement followed rather similar lines with greater success. For an older age group the YMCA expanded very rapidly, almost trebling its member associations in the ten years to 1894. School boards attacked the problem through evening schools. After virtually disappearing in the 1870s and early 1880s these recovered, partly because of the demand for technical instruction, which is not directly relevant here, but also through the efforts of pressure groups devoted to recreational education. The Recreative Evening Schools Association, for example, very active in London and elsewhere in the 1880s, encouraged classes in physical education, choral and instrumental music, handicrafts and similar activities, arranging publicity and paying instructors, a very necessary function in the absence of any support from the Education Department. Some school boards conducted full-scale crusades to encourage enrolment, organizing social evenings and other entertainments, and attempting to hold students together while the schools were closed in summer by sponsoring outings, sports events and so on. In certain particularly deprived areas experiments were made in opening schools for an evening or two each week, allowing children of any age to come in for games, reading and refreshment. It would be idle to pretend that these efforts achieved conspicuous success. Few school boards or local education authorities showed the sustained zeal necessary to make progress in this disheartening field, and even where provision was most extensive, evening school superintendents were uneasily aware that they were hardly scratching the surface of the problem. As is so often the case, they were preaching to the converted. Their institutes and clubs provided useful facilities for young people interested enough to make use of them—and this was in itself a valuable service—but the customers they really wanted to attract stayed away. However, in the context of this study, the success or failure of the movement for recreational education is less important than the powerful support which it attracted. A belief had taken firm root that young people needed to be provided with rational entertainment, and that this must be structured and institutionalized. Already titles such as 'extension' and 'continuation' classes were being used, implying that provision for young people was seen as a development of schooling, even if the content and techniques were rather different.

It is not necessary to follow in detail the development of the themes initiated in the period from 1890-1914. Schemes of continuative education occupied important places in both the Fisher Act of 1918 and the Butler Act of 1944, even if concrete results of the legislation have been depressingly meagre, while youth work, particularly in its official forms, has made major strides since 1945. In this connection it is interesting to observe how the relationship between schools and the youth service has become closer. In a way, this is an inevitable result of the rising school leaving age, which brings into schools an increasing proportion of pupils who must be classed as 'youth' rather than 'children'. But deliberate policy has also played a part. Youth centres are often attached to schools, making use of gymnasia, stages and other school amenities, while appointments of teacher/youth leaders are made with the expressed intention of encouraging pupils to join the centres' activities both during and after their school career. At the same time schools have increasingly tended to interest themselves in the leisure time activities of their pupils, joining in such schemes as the Duke of Edinburgh's Award, which may well continue after pupils have left school.

This rapprochement between school and youth service is part of a wider tendency, very apparent since the Second World War, for the traditionally fairly distinct boundaries between school and society to become blurred. This is evident, for instance, in the campaign to abandon academic subjects and devise curricula 'relevant' to the pupils' interests, 'relevance', so far as the word is not used merely as a slogan, being measured in terms of the presumed present or future activities of the pupils outside school. It can, however, be pressed very much further, involving a deliberate engagement of pupils, usually but not necessarily older pupils, in social work or in investigating their local community. The reverse process is also possible. The community may be brought into the school as in the Cambridgeshire village colleges which have been copied with more or less variation in many areas, where the school is used as a centre for adult and youth classes, clubs societies, meetings and community events of all kinds. Among the hoped for side-effects are increased pupil motivation, enrolment of present and former pupils in classes and societies, and a higher degree of adult interest and co-operation in school affairs. In the community school, strongly advocated at the present time, efforts are made to combine the two processes in a two-way interpenetration of school and community. In all such schemes, education is seen as a process continuing long after the normal school leaving age, and involving far more than the traditional academic curriculum. They are of consequence to us because they reflect, not only the continuous lengthening of the proportion of a person's life spent in education, but also the belief that this period should be spent in, or at least in continual contact with, institutions of formal learning, and that it should be subject to a high degree of professional supervision.

The extension of the school's brief into what were formerly considered to be private affairs may be illustrated by another recent development, the appearance of the school counsellor. Counselling began in a fairly innocuous and uncontroversial way with careers advice to school leavers, but the scope of the advice has been extended to include every kind of academic, vocational and personal problem, and a new profession of school counsellor has been established. Musgrove and Taylor argue (1969, p.11) that this is a most sinister innovation, providing the school with a tool of indoctrination of immense power against the influence of parents. Whether or not this is the case it is certainly true that the school counsellor is assuming roles played in the past by parents, priests and family doctor. Of course, some teachers, chiefly in boarding schools, have in the past played a not too dissimilar part, but they did this on the basis of personal influence, not of professional right. Schools may be justified in offering a counselling service—it is not the function of this study to examine the question—but in doing so they are certainly widening their brief as it has normally been understood.

Chapter 2

The concepts of 'childhood' and 'youth'

The rise of formal schooling as the dominant educational agency was accompanied by a revolution in attitudes towards childhood, so fundamental as to make it almost reasonable to say that childhood was invented in the eighteenth and nineteenth centuries. Obviously there have always been members of society who fell within the age range now associated with childhood, but it is surprising to people used to modern thinking how little special attention was paid to them. We live in a child-centred society where the importance of allowing children to follow their interests and develop their individual potential—at great cost to the community at large—is taken for granted. Perhaps, indeed, we take it too much for granted. Ivan Illich in *De-schooling Society* talks of the necessity to end 'the present discrimination against infants, adults, and the old in favour of children' (Illich, 1971, p.28) and, whether or not one subscribes to his general views, one must admit that he has a point here. It may be that we have found the right balance between the value placed on infancy, childhood, youth, adulthood and old age, but this is not self-evident, and there may be dangers in supposing that it is. The question has, in fact, been posed quite recently whether the balance should not be shifted in favour of the aged, whose interests may be ignored in an age dedicated to youth values. And, as in the case of the development of schooling, the child-centred society is a comparatively new phenomenon. Its origins may be traced to the sixteenth or even fifteenth centuries, but the critical change, and here again the parallel with schooling is close, occurred at the turn of the eighteenth and nineteenth centuries.

In all societies a stage of infancy is recognized, and in most this time is spent at home in close dependence upon the mother, or at least upon a restricted family group. It is in respect of the years

27

following infancy that modern industrial societies differ from their predecessors. In pre-industrial England, children, with very few exceptions, were taken as soon as they were old enough to leave their mothers, and placed as trainees in an adult society. It was recognized, of course, that they were small, weak and ignorant, but nevertheless they were *in* society as proto-adults, and not separated from it in distinctly child-orientated institutions. As one ascended the social scale there was a tendency for the age at which children began training to rise, but still, even aristocratic children entered some nobleman's house at an age when their modern descendants would be at preparatory school. The only group exempted from apprenticeship, in theory at least, were the clergy, and even their education at grammar school and university began very early and was strictly vocational in nature.

It is worthwhile briefly to consider the assumptions underlying pre-industrial apprenticeship because of the light such an examination throws upon contemporary attitudes towards childhood and education. Ideally, apprenticeship was a one-to-one relationship between master and pupil, and although this relationship was probably seldom achieved, the number of pupils per master was very small, and the master's job was only incidentally that of teacher. His prime function was that of craftsman, merchant, knight or whatever, and his apprentices were all at some point along the route towards mastery of the trade. The whole process was adult-orientated. The apprentices were learning an adult activity, their success was measured against adult standards, and the culminating point was achievement of full adult status as member of a guild. In point of fact, many apprentices never did attain membership of a guild, but this is merely an early example of the failure of educational practice to live up to the theories upon which it is based. There was no notion that childhood might be a stage of life with interests and activities which had their own value and deserved to be encouraged for their own sake. Rather the opposite, since in so far as specifically childhood activities were recognized, they were regarded as a hindrance to the rapid achievement of maturity, and therefore to be discouraged. At best they might be accepted grudgingly as necessary evils, as a degree of boisterousness and high spirits among apprentices was taken for granted. But childhood interests as a whole were 'childish', and the word had a definitely pejorative connotation. A child who transcended the pursuits typical of his age was regarded with an approbation about which most modern parents and teachers would have strong reservations. Some children acquired a quantity of adult learning puzzling to a post-Piaget generation. St Mary's church in Nottingham has a memorial to Henry Plumptre who died at ten years of age in 1718 (Pinchbeck and Hewitt, 1970, p.271) 'In those few tender years he had to a great degree made himself master of the Jewish, Roman and English history, the Heathen mythology and the French tongue, and was not inconsiderably advanced in Latin.' It is recorded that John Evelyn's son, Richard, could read English, French, Latin and 'Gothic' at two-and-a-half, and at five could 'not only read most written hands, but so decline all the nounes, conjugate the verbs regular and most of the irregular . . . could make congruous syntax, turne English into Latin, and vice versa . . . and had a strange passion for Greeke . . . he had learned all his Catechism early and understood the historical part of the Bible and New Testament.' Other children, while perhaps less well informed, showed a wholly precocious maturity of manner, like young George Holles, who at two years, was (Pinchbeck and Hewitt, 1970, p.270) 'full of life and spirit which yet had a mixture of mildness and gravity, and he would many times suddainly (sic) step aside from the height of his little sportes and (kneeling against the wall) whould say his prayers.'

The modern reaction to such anecdotes is to exclaim 'how unnatural!' and to regret that these little prodigies should grow into adults without ever being children. But this response precisely illustrates the gulf between our view of childhood and that of seventeenth-century parents. To them childhood was a state of incomplete adulthood, an inevitable but unfortunate period of weakness to be crossed as quickly as possible. The suggestion that a child might grow up too quickly would seem quite absurd; a child's function was to grow up.

The same attitude persisted when one moved from the technical to the moral sphere, and apprenticeship was taken to be as much a method of moral and social initiation as of technical training. The master was in a very real sense *in loco parentis*, responsible for his apprentices' misdemeanours and entitled to punish them. Appeal against the authority of the master was very difficult, and it seems that even parents had very little redress where a master was concerned, although corporate bodies such as charity schools did sometimes intervene successfully on behalf of former pupils who were maltreated by masters. The morality which was inculcated, whether by parent or master, was an adult code laying great emphasis upon the duty of children to respect and obey their elders. Again, childhood was seen as a period of weakness when one was specially prone to temptation, but there was no notion that children might not comprehend moral questions, or, at least, any such lack of comprehension was attributed to unusual stupidity or lack of attention The common belief in original sin reinforced this view. Children, it was held, had an inbuilt tendency to succumb to temptation, which could only be kept in check by a strict discipline, In childhood this discipline had to be external, but it was hoped that with training and application it would be internalized, such internalization being the mark of an adult. Since, in this theory, childhood was not merely a stage of moral dependence but also a period when one was peculiarly susceptible to sin, it is not surprising that the common view was that the faster children grew up the better. The doctrine of original sin goes some way to explain the treatment of children, which, by modern standards was often harsh to the point of brutality. By a historical accident this doctrine was strongly supported in the eighteenth century, notably by the Methodists, and may have delayed the effect of changes in attitudes to children which were gathering force at this time.

The concept of childhood as a stage having characteristic needs and interests which have a value of their own, regardless of their role in preparing for adult life, began to appear in England in the sixteenth and seventeenth centuries. At first it took the form of the provision of facilities specifically for children. The appearance of nuclear families had much to do with this. As the family separated itself from servants and retainers, children of the family came to form a distinct category with its own role and status. At the same time, the greater frequency with which the family met as a unit apart from the rest of the household encouraged more intimate relationships to develop between parent and child. The proportion of the population which was sent to school increased, while in those families where children were still educated at home it became increasingly usual for the teaching to be done by professional tutors and governesses. This was an important development for, while a master craftsman's function was only incidentally that of training apprentices, teachers and tutors were engaged solely with children.

Economic problems provided another reason for interest in childhood. Both private persons and public authorities were much concerned about unemployment, which made itself unpleasantly apparent in the shape of wandering bands of 'sturdy beggars' who were inclined to encourage contributions from the towns and villages through which they passed by means of violence or intimidation. Most of this unemployment was due to rising population and changes in agricultural techniques but, as is so often the case, public opinon preferred to attribute it to moral deficiencies on the part of the unemployed. Since it was fully appreciated that children are more easy to influence than their elders, it seemed sensible to attack the problem by means of a campaign directed against the children, and fairly frequent experiments were made in running industrial schools, combining a measure of rudimentary instruction with hard work under strict discipline which, it was hoped, would inculcate habits of thrift and industry. An added attraction of these schools was that they promised to pay for themselves, or even make a profit from the children's work.

The seventeenth century was fertile in educational schemes. It is not necessary at this point to consider why this was so, but the fact is clear enough. In addition to the industrial schools, very often offshoots of the Poor Law, many charity schools were established, the culmination coming right at the end of the century with the campaign directed by the Society for Propagating Christian Knowledge. Grammar schools flourished too, and one of the consequences of the religious disputes of the period was the establishment, after 1660, of numerous Dissenting academies, which played a conspicuous part in secondary and higher education for the next hundred and fifty years. Education was very much a matter of public discussion. The writings of John Amos Comenius were vigorously debated in this country at the time of the Protectorate and Restoration. Among numerous English writers on education at least three, Bacon, Milton and Locke were indisputably in the first rank. By 1700 childhood was becoming established as a stage in life which presented peculiar problems, but also, for the educator or propagandist, peculiar opportunities. Realization of this did not yet extend very far, but major figures in philosophy, science and letters were exercising their minds on the topic.

But, although the beginnings of a shift in attitude can be detected earlier, really dramatic change came in the eighteenth century, and is associated with Rousseau and the Romantic movement. Rousseau and his followers turned the doctrine of original sin upside down, maintaining that children, far from being innately sinful, are born in a state of innocence, and only become corrupted by contact with society which is the real source of sin. This was not an entirely novel argument. Various seventeenth-century writers may be quoted who denied the doctrine of original sin, and the English philosopher Shaftesbury even produced an early version of the noble savage, writing of 'that simplicity and innocence of behaviour which has often been known among mere savages ere they were corrupted by our commerce' (Coveney, 1967, pp.42f). But it was in the late eighteenth century that this new attitude began to command general support, and to influence the upbringing and education of children. Childhood as a phenomenon now became an object of fashionable interest, and methods of instruction and discipline received a more searching investigation. Domestic education enjoyed a period of renewed popularity reflecting parental concern over their children's welfare, and although few were prepared to follow Rousseau's precepts too far in the direction of disciplinary permissiveness, many teachers, through conviction or parental pressure, searched for alternatives to the ubiquitous corporal punishment of earlier days. Lancaster and Bell, for example, agreed in opposing corporal punishment, and Lancaster produced complicated alternative schemes, generally involving public applause or humiliation.

But Rousseau's influence extended further than merely the amelioration of discipline. The traditional view of mental growth may be described with fair accuracy as a process of summation. A child started with no concepts at all, his mind a blank sheet—*tabula rasa*. His experiences were stored in his mind in a more or less automatic manner, and experiences which were related causally, or in time, or in certain other ways, formed patterns, a teacher's work very largely consisting of so regulating his pupils' experiences that the right patterns were formed. Two important features of this psychology, from our point of view, were: first, that the mind was a passive machine for storing impressions, having no inbuilt tendency to organize the information provided for it and capable of more or less infinite variation according to the quantity and quality of information received; and second, that the concepts formed by a child were in all essentials identical to those formed by an adult. The only reason for a child's failure to understand, let us say, a problem

in mathematics, or an ethical dilemma, was lack of relevant information. This psychology received its classical statement from Locke
at the end of the seventeenth century, and was refined during the
next hundred years, notably by the French philosopher Helvetius
and the English psychologist Hartley. But it has always been, as it
still is, the layman's psychology. In 1762, however, in his *Émile*
Rousseau produced a clear account of what is, in outline at any rate,
the modern concept of human development. He maintained that a
child grows to adulthood, not by a gradual, unbroken process of
accretion, but by a periodic movement through certain distinct
stages. In contrast to the traditional view, the mind was thought of
as actively organizing the information it received, and at each stage
of development it had characteristic modes of organization. At one
stage, Rousseau maintained, sensual experience is particularly
important, later a child becomes capable of intellectual understanding
and analytic reasoning, and later again he is able to comprehend
moral and aesthetic questions. These stages follow one another in
an individual's development in a fixed order, and if a child is to move
from one stage to another, he must first acquire a full competence in
the mode of understanding peculiar to the stage at which he now
stands. Thus, if a young child is deprived of the opportunity of
sensory exploration of his environment his development to the intellectual and moral stages may be delayed, or even in extreme cases
prevented.

Now, the consequences of accepting Rousseau's psychology are
fairly obvious. The notion that a child is merely a small adult
becomes untenable. His manner of thinking and understanding is
quite different from an adult's, and what to an adult appears logical
may to a child appear meaningless or quite arbitrary. Furthermore,
it becomes very important that a parent or teacher who wishes to
bring a child up to be a successful adult must first allow—even
encourage—him to be a child. To attempt to short-circuit the process
will result in producing a person who is chronologically adult, but
intellectually and morally childish. In fact, developmental psychology
did not make much progress among teachers in this country until
the twentieth century, associationism based upon Locke's idea
holding the field quite firmly. But, if teaching methods were not
much affected, developmental psychology did much to strengthen
the growing belief that children were not just little adults, and provided a theoretical structure for this opinion which was to be

reinforced from different directions by Spencer and Hall a hundred years later.

The Romantic movement was also influential in making the turn of the eighteenth and nineteenth centuries critical in the development of a new concept of childhood. Many Romantics, of course, were committed admirers of Rousseau. They joined with him in placing a high value on spontaneity rather than upon analysis and reasoning, and a correspondingly low value on knowledge and experience, especially where this was gained at second hand through books. They also accepted his belief in the natural innocence of children, and maintained that in growing up, a child lost not only this innocence, but also his original directness of response both to people and to nature. Their interest in childhood was demonstrated by the fact that the first literary treatment of the subject appeared at this time in Blake's *Songs of Innocence* and Wordsworth's 'Ode on Intimations of Immortality'. An indication of the way in which the new concept was gaining acceptance is that the first books written specially for children also appeared in the last quarter of the eighteenth century, together with children's clothes, although these were still generally considered an affectation.

There is some evidence of a reaction against some of the more advanced 'progressive' views on child-rearing after about 1815. It may be that radical ideas were discredited by their association with the French Revolution, but more important was the contemporary moral revolution in this country. In Professor Perkin's words (1969, p.280):

> Between 1780 and 1850 the English ceased to be one of the most aggressive, brutal, rowdy, outspoken, riotous, cruel and bloodthirsty nations in the world, and became one of the most inhibited, polite, orderly, tender-minded, prudish and hypocritical.

One effect of this was that youthful peccadilloes were regarded with less tolerance, the belief in original sin making a strong recovery. The campaign against corporal punishment seems to have lost much of its impetus, while the revival of the public schools involved a deliberate tightening of discipline and a concentration on the social and moral aspects of education quite foreign to the anarchic traditions of eighteenth-century public schools. The greater readiness shown by parents at this time to send their children away to boarding school may have been due, in part at least, to their belief that boys needed the stern discipline of the revived public school to fit them for the struggle against their innate sinfulness. Certainly, a stress on character-building and moral stamina is one of the most character-istic features of the reforms of Arnold and his followers.

But this reversion to a disciplinary concept of education went along with a continued concern for childhood, and may indeed have been a symptom of it. Another sympton was the extensive use of children as a subject for literature. It was in the 1830s and 1840s that the first novels were written which took children as their central characters. One thinks immediately of Dickens in this connection, but although he was certainly the master of the genre, he had many notable rivals—Marryat, Kingsley, Frances Trollope and Charlotte Yonge to name only the most distinguished. Particularly significant in Dickens' books is the way in which he used the death of children to play on his readers' emotions. *Oliver Twist, Nicholas Nickleby, The Old Curiosity Shop, Dombey and Son, Our Mutual Friend*, all have set piece death bed scenes deliberately designed as a focus for sentiment and pathos. The immense success of his books makes clear to us the degree to which children had become a symbol of innocence. And although Dickens undoubtedly did much to crystal-lize such feelings and bring them into consciousness, he was exploit-ing feelings which already existed. As Philip Collins observes (1963, p.178): 'Even Dickens' huge literary talent could not have imposed these death bed scenes on an unwilling public.'

So far we have been concerned with tracing shifts of opinion which, while they produced fundamental changes in attitudes towards children and in methods of child-rearing and education, worked through their effects on individual parents and teachers, so that generalizations about their total effect are difficult to make. But in the nineteenth century there was a new development—legislation specifically for the protection of children. The Factory Acts pointed the way by distinguishing in their clauses between adult men, women and children, but of more significance in this context were the measures which gave children protection against their parents. Cruelty towards children was an issue which caused the Victorians much concern because, while they were fully aware that parents were frequently responsible for cruelty, either through active ill-treatment or more commonly through neglect of their responsibilities, to inter-fere with a parent's authority ran counter to some of their most firmly held convictions. It is a measure of the depth to which public opinion was stirred by repeated revelations of ill-treatment that the government was able and willing to act. In a sense, of course, the Factory Acts were directed against parents since they limited the circumstances under which children could be sent out to work. The introduction of compulsory schooling in 1876 was another major inroad upon parents' freedom. But in the 1880s the government went further by producing laws explicitly designed to prevent ill-treatment of children by their parents. Acts of 1880 and 1889 gave the courts power to act in cases of active brutality by parents, and under the latter Act they could remove children from their parents' control. By an addition to this Act, police were allowed to take children into care without a court order where cruelty was only suspected, and in 1904 the same powers were extended to inspectors of the National Society for the Prevention of Cruelty to Children. In comparison with the situation obtained at the beginning of the nineteenth century, these were astonishing limitations upon parental power, but mention of the NSPCC illustrates the powerful public pressure which supported these measures. The first society for the prevention of child cruelty was formed in Liverpool in 1883 and the NSPCC followed six years later, receiving a Royal Charter in 1895.

Meanwhile important developments were occurring in the psychological field. Associationism remained the dominant school in English psychology almost until the end of the century, and its rather crude rules for the association of ideas were refined and made more comprehensive, notably by Alexander Bain in the 1850s. But it was attacked from several directions with increasing effect. One powerful assault was delivered from the standpoint of evolution by Herbert Spencer. He revived the concept of stages of psychological development, which he linked to the development of the central nervous system, and enunciated the 'recapitulation' theory, by which humans are supposed to reproduce in their individual maturation the stages through which the species has passed in the process of evolution. Both these theories emphasized the autonomy of childhood as a stage of human development, a point which Spencer urged quite explicitly in his *Principles of Psychology*, published in 1855. Recapitulation was taken up some fifty years later by the American psychologist Stanley Hall as the basis for his influential study of adolescence. In the 1880s, further attacks came from a group of psychologists and philosophers who were influenced by German thinkers, including T. H. Green who was also a political philosopher of major importance, and James Ward who produced what amounted to a manifesto in the *Encyclopaedia Britannica* of 1886. This school rejected the mechanical features of associationism, seeing the mind as active in its interpretation of experience in the manner of Rousseau, and likewise accepting the concept of stages of development. By the end of the century the hold of associationism was visibly crumbling, and a sign of this was the appearance of child psychology, a recognition that the child's mind was different from and not just smaller than the adults. W. T. Preyer, a German, is considered to have founded the subject with his book *The Mind of the Child* of 1881, and by 1900, journals and associations for child study had been established in various European countries and in the USA where it was taken up with enthusiasm.

By the beginning of this century, therefore, childhood had been definitely established as an autonomous stage in human development, with its own mode of thinking, its own interests, and with legislation protecting it from cruelty and exploitation by adults. It was spent, not in communities of adults, but in special child-orientated institutions supervised by professional teachers. The autonomy of childhood was carried to an extreme by 'progressive' teachers who argued that their function was not simply to prepare their pupils for adult life, but rather to allow them to express their interests as children. Many such teachers, it is true, adopted this approach believing it to be the most effective way of encouraging social and intellectual growth, but the point was firmly pressed that children's activities and interests were valuable in themselves, and not merely as a means to the end of maturation.

The next development was the recognition of another developmental stage, this time intermediate between childhood and adulthood. 'Youth' was not, of course, an invention of the twentieth century. Young men of the wealthy classes had always been allowed a period of time to work out their high spirits before settling down to a career or to running the estate, and a traditional licence had been allowed to university students. Apprentices, too, were a notoriously rowdy group, and their antics generally received a measure of tolerance. But the great mass of the population had no youth as they had no childhood. At the age of fifteen or sixteen they had long been employed full-time and were, indeed, very often at the peak of their earning career, few having any prospect of advancement and most facing falling incomes as their physical powers declined. When a working class child entered employment he became a young adult, and there was no provision of clubs or societies specifically aimed at this age group. In fact there seems to have been virtually no realization of the existence of any individual or social problems peculiar to youth. Children, as we have seen, were the objects of immense philanthropic efforts, and eventually of protective legislation. Women, as a group with special difficulties, attracted attention. Some of the Factory Acts had clauses relating to the employment of women, and a start was made in removing their legal disabilities. But practically the only recognition of youth as a separate category appears in some of the official reports and Factory Acts, where 'young persons' are occasionally referred to, the dividing line between children and young persons often being drawn at thirteen years. Frequently, however, even these sources speak of 'children and young persons' in one phrase as if they shared common problems.

Public opinion really began to take notice of youth as a social problem in the 1880s, and the stimulus seems to have come from an awareness that the disciplinary results achieved by the new board schools, remarkable as they were to those acquainted with their intake, were often depressingly short-lived, their alumni reverting to disorder and shiftlessness almost as soon as the control of the teacher was removed. The appearance of youth movements and continuation evening classes, as well as pressure to raise the school-leaving age, were all responses to concern about the awkward gap which was now seen to exist between leaving school and settling down to adult life, a gap very often filled by activities which were either actively lawless or anti-social, or only too obviously unproductive and time-wasting. And at the end of the nineteenth century, when self-help and self-improvement were taken very seriously, the accusation of time-wasting carried more sting than it does today when 'dropping-out' is defended as a virtue and the 'rat-race' is a dirty word.

Although youth is such a new discovery it was established very quickly as a recognized social phenomenon. But although it was accepted almost immediately as an autonomous stage of development, it is in the last few years, certainly since 1945, that it came to be seen as producing major problems—economic, moral, political, legal, and particularly educational. It is probably true to say that problems of youth have attracted more attention recently than have problems of childhood. In part, of course, this is due to the way in which youth, like childhood in earlier days, has expanded both up and down the age range. The concept of 'youth' has always been a nebulous one, its boundaries shifting confusingly in different contexts, and very often all we can say is that it lies between childhood and adulthood, and we have already noted how the boundaries of childhood have changed from time to time. In this context we can narrow the concept a little at any rate. For, until recently—and this is a point to which we shall have to return—it has not been usual to refer to a pupil at school as a youth. Nor does one as a rule want to speak of a young man of twenty-two or twenty-three as a youth. It is probably fair to say that youth has generally been taken to describe the period from when a child leaves school to about twenty-one years of age, which, until recently was the legal age at which adulthood began. Even this allows problems to creep in since children leave school at various ages, but the youth service takes as its brief, young people between fourteen and twenty-one years, and this definition would be accepted for most purposes with the addition that pupils in school did not come into this category.

In the last few years the situation has become more complicated. The tendency from the 1870s, when compulsory schooling was instituted, until the 1960s was for the lower boundary of the youth stage to be pressed upwards as the school-leaving age rose, while the upper limit remained more or less constant. Throughout this period it remained the assumption that in speaking of youth, one was referring to young people who were not in full-time education. School children were not included at one end, nor were university or training college students, and this accounted for virtually the whole of the higher education sector. Three important changes have occurred very recently, so recently that their implications are not yet really clear. First, the proportion of the age group in higher education has vastly increased, and this very large group is now included within the definition of youth. Indeed it is very apparent that most of the more articulate youth leaders are drawn from past or present students. In the past, students have sometimes sought solidarity with the working class, but it is a new turn for them to see themselves—and to be accepted—as leaders of an age group. Second, and this is very new, a tendency has appeared to separate the upper parts of schools, treating the older pupils, as a matter of policy, as youth rather than as children. Thus we have the establishment of sixth form colleges and of ROSLA units, often furnished and equipped very differently from the conventional school. That this tendency is in line with the thinking of pupils themselves is suggested by the increasing number of pupils who leave school to take 'O' and 'A' levels in colleges of further education, often expressly in search of a less child-orientated environment. Third, the upper boundary of youth has been extended, and it is very obvious to any observer of the youth scene that the leaders of opinion are generally to be found among people who would not, even ten years ago, have been considered as youth at all.

All these changes are clearly related to the maturation of youth as a group with a conscious independent existence. An embryo stratification of society on the basis of age is not altogether new. Some of the Romantics were conscious of themselves as young rebels. Something of a youth cult existed in the 1890s, consciously revolting against established standards in art, literature and morality. After the First World War there was much talk of the young having been let down by 'old men'. But these manifestations were all short-lived and confined to a relatively small group of intellectuals. The establishment of a national—indeed in aspiration international—youth culture is a development of the post-1945 era, and particularly of the 1960s. It may be that the unity of this culture is more apparent than real, and might fracture under stress of political or racial tensions like several experiments in international socialism; but appeals to youth solidarity do produce a response, and certain leaders do regard themselves as spokesmen for the culture, and command a following. It is not surprising that some of these continue to represent, or claim to represent, the age group long after their chronological age places them firmly in the ranks of the enemy.

The youth sector has inherited a number of problems formerly characteristic of childhood, many of which are related to the increased proportion of the age group in full-time institutional education. What does one teach? Is education to be conceived as initiation into a body of knowledge, or as development of individual potential, or as following consumer demand for training in marketable skills? How far does one go in the direction of student participation, or student control? How does one arouse motivation to learn? These questions, long debated in schools, now centre upon higher education, and the backwash of decisions reached in this sector is beginning to work its way into school. When the very limited numbers in higher education were all motivated either by intellectual curiosity or by ambitions for enhanced career prospects, such questions attracted little attention. But now when many in the age group are in college, school or university either through compulsion or through simply following the herd with very little commitment, either academic or vocational, they loom very large indeed, and are exacerbated by the fact that youth, relative to children, is mature and articulate in the complaints.

Youth has inherited another feature from childhood: its use as a stalking horse by social and political commentators. In educational writing and in literature generally, the child has frequently occupied a role somewhat similar to that of the noble savage. One misses much of the significance of 'progressive' writers, from Rousseau to Illich, if one fails to take account of the fact that their educational doctrines are only part of a wider social philosophy; in most cases the point is made explicitly by the writers themselves. Characteristically, the arguments of these writers move on two levels. When Rousseau speaks of the innocence of childhood he is making an assertion about child psychology which, if true, has important educational implications; but he is also using the 'natural', uncorrupted child much as Swift used the Lilliputians, or William Morris used the medieval peasants and craftsmen, as a device to throw into relief the corruption and insincerity of adult society. In this sense the literal truth of his assertions is almost irrelevant compared with their effect in jolting readers into looking again at activities and assumptions which have, by usage, come to be accepted unquestioningly. Current assertions about radical youth, with its rejection of hypocritical bourgeois morality, its refusal to join the rat-race, its love of peace and tolerance, have to be interpreted in a rather similar way, less perhaps as statements about what young people *are*, than as descriptions of how adult life would look to a person who had not yet been brainwashed into accepting the assumptions upon which it rests. Here we have one of the reasons for the apparent enthusiasm for the youth culture of radical thinkers who are clearly adults; they are using a time-honoured and respectable technique of social criticism.

They may also be affected by a sentiment which has an equally long pedigree, and which similarly has been transferred from childhood to youth. Nostalgia for the carelessness of childhood, with its lack of concern for the future, and its absence of the responsibilities of parenthood and vocation, occurs in literature at least as early as

Shakespeare. References to it are common in eighteenth-century and Romantic literature, notably in Gray's 'Ode on a Distant Prospect of Eton College', and in Wordsworth, and E. C. Mack (1938, pp.45f.) has pointed out how memoirs of nineteenth-century schooling were almost invariably seen through a sentimental haze. The relationship of such nostalgic memoirs to reality is questionable, but the existence of this idealized recollection of childhood is too well documented and too much a matter of common experience to be doubted. Recently, this nostalgia has become attached to youth rather than to childhood. It is youth, we are told, that lives for the day, drops out, and joins the fun-culture, and the attractions of this life, however chimerical, to the middle-aged, harrassed by mortgages, hire-purchases, and the threat of redundancy, is perfectly obvious. Then again, the middle-aged, uneasily aware that they have compromised with their own consciences, can find some wish-fulfilling consolation in identifying with young rebels.

Without doubt one of the most potent factors in the establishment of youth as an independent age group has been commercial exploitation. To business interests after the Second World War, youth represented a very attractive field for enterprise. In the past it had been only lightly cultivated, partly because it had very little spending power, and partly because its choice of goods tended to be supervised by adults so that a direct appeal to its tastes was of little commercial advantage. But since 1945 its purchasing power has risen sharply, more sharply than that of the population at large, and even those young people who have no independent income receive much larger allowances from their parents. At the same time, parents and others in authority have become more reluctant to interfere with young people's choice, and the marketers have been able to take full advantage of the fact that youth, for all the talk about its critical attitude and rejection of authority, is in hard fact particularly susceptible to advertising, especially where this plays on the need to conform to peer group expectations. So we have the appearance of industries specifically aimed at the manipulation and exploitation of the youth market. The most obvious manifestations of this are in popular entertainment, dress, and cosmetics, where the stratification of taste on the basis of age is very clear.

The effect of commercial activities in crystallizing the youth culture has been only partly planned. Promoters have, of course, worked hard and deliberately to build up group solidarity and to use it to increase sales. In pursuit of this end they have produced stereotypes of 'young man' and 'young woman' to which they can then persuade their customers to conform, changing the sterotypes from time to time sufficiently to allow for planned obsolescence. And they have, with equal calculation, created cult heroes with whom their customers may identify. So far there is nothing very novel about the situation; these are long serving advertising techniques, perhaps deployed with more than usual pertinacity and professional skill. But they have been working on very fertile soil. It is hard to believe that a youth culture could have emerged so rapidly in the 1960s unless a latent consciousness of age stratification had not already existed to be exploited. Propagandists and advertisers must promise to satisfy some need in their audience, however that need is later used or perverted. And it does seem as if a division of society on the basis of age has something of the attraction for the mid-twentieth century that a division on the basis of social class had for the early nineteenth. For youth is not the only age group which has shown signs of independent existence since 1945. We have heard much about the special problems of the old, a group which shares with women and children the distinction of being subject to special legislation. If one looks critically at advertisements, particularly, perhaps, those aimed at men, one can see that a campaign, rather muted as yet, is being waged to appeal to that group which lies between youth on the one hand and middle age on the other. It is instructive in this connection to look at the stereotype of manliness offered to the young man in the youth category with that offered to the man ten years his senior. In part, the contrast arises simply from the differential spending power of the two groups, but it extends further than merely offering similar goods at different prices. It assumes very different life styles with, for the older group, much emphasis upon career success. The image held before this group for identification is not the folk singer or the entertainer, but the rising executive; grooming, dress, and conspicuous expenditure rate high in the offered scale of values.

Exploitation may be political as well as commercial, and here again the 1960s have seen the emergence of youth as an independent power—if power is the right word in this context. The effect is not so widespread—political inertia is a phenomenon common to all age groups—and it appears at present to be confined chiefly to the student element. In politics, as in commerce, one uses the word 'exploitation' advisedly here since, although political activism has had an important effect in producing group consciousness in youth, it is very apparent that political movements are generally instigated by older contemporaries, or, very often, by leaders well outside the age group. For instance, unrest in universities and colleges is frequently fomented by junior members of staff and by postgraduate students, while the recent extension of this unrest to schools has quite explicitly been advocated and aroused by student activists, again supported by junior members of staff. In both cases, the Leninist technique is used of the cadre of activists exploiting the assumed support of the largely inert mass; the variation here being that in many cases the members of the cadres, while within the institution to be attacked, are outside the group which is being agitated.

So we have, reaching maturity in the twentieth century, the concept of childhood and youth as separate, autonomous stages in life, with their own interests and activities having value intrinsically, and not merely as preparation for adult life. A child, it is argued, and here the contrast with the old dispensation is particularly clear, should be childish, and not be pressed into becoming too quickly an adult; and the same, with the necessary amendments, is true of youth. As we have seen, various lines of thought converge on this point, and one must read with care to see whether the preparatory, or disciplinary concept of education is being attacked (a) because it is, in fact, inefficient as a preparation; or (b) because childhood or youth activities have value in themselves; or (c) because adult society is corrupt, and preparation for it is therefore morally wrong. It will be necessary to look more closely at each of these approaches in later chapters, but it is enough for now that they reinforce one another in underlining the autonomy of childhood and youth. At the same time there occurred the development noticed in chapter 1, by which a rapidly increasing proportion of children and young people is engaged in full-time institutional education. This in turn was accompanied by a widening of the brief of education, involving the organization and institutionalization of many activities previously left to private venture or to such semi-official bodies as the Church. The question which occurs to us is, what is the relationship between these phenomena? Their chronological coincidence, and their effect upon the same age groups entitle us to suppose, *prima facie*, that some relationship does exist.

Advocates of 'de-schooling' have a straightforward answer to this question. The relationship, they argue, is one of cause and effect. Modern educational systems are a product of urban industrial society, and one of their prime, if undeclared, functions is to condition their pupils into accepting the (Illich, 1971, p.28) 'myth of unending consumption', or in other words, into believing that civilization progresses by the constant accretion of goods and services to satisfy material wants. These school systems have the characteristics of being age-specific, obligatory and monopolistic. They have (Illich, 1971, p.34) 'a monopoly on both the resources of learning and the investiture of social roles', and 'select for each successive level those who have, at earlier stages in the game, proved themselves good risks for the established order.' They are self-perpetuating because they institutionalize their pupils, rendering them dependent upon institutional help, and unable even to visualize the possibility of independent learning (Illich, 1971, pp.2, 3):

> Rich and poor alike, depend on schools and hospitals which guide their lives, form their world view, and define for them what is legitimate and what is not. Both view doctoring oneself as irresponsible, learning on one's own as unreliable, and community organization, when not paid for by those in authority, as a form of aggression or subversion. For both groups the reliance upon institutional treatment renders independent achievement suspect.

A side-effect of the establishment of compulsory monopolistic educational systems is the appearance of stratification according to age, and of the problems which go with it. Schools and colleges isolate an age range from adult society in establishments devoted to the interests of that age range, giving rise to a group consciousness, the reverse of which, frequently, is a kind of xenophobic rejection of the values of other cultures and age groups. To quote Illich again (1971, p.28) 'If there were no age-specific, obligatory learning institutions "childhood" would go out of production. The youth of rich nations would be liberated from its destructiveness.'

Now this argument has not so far aroused much serious interest in this country, which is indeed in the process of extending the period of obligatory institutional education to eleven years, and where a campaign is building up for extension at the lower age limit. So it is worth while to point out that, whether or not we finally accept its analysis as adequate, there is nothing about it which is self-evidently absurd. In fact a respectable body of evidence can be marshalled in its defence. Pinchbeck and Hewitt (1970, p.21) have suggested that one of the factors leading to the emergence of childhood in the sixteenth and seventeenth centuries was the beginning of the replacement of apprenticeship by schooling, involving collecting children together in child-orientated institutions apart from adult society. The plausibility of this contention is increased by a consideration of the way in which the gathering together of large masses of the working class in industrial towns in the early nineteenth century helped to produce an autonomous working class consciousness. One may speculate whether the rise of student protest in the 1960s was not associated with the very rapid rise in student numbers which was taking place at the same time, producing relatively large, self-contained enclaves of students, with a sense of identity, common purpose and, of course, strength. The capacity of such insulated institutions as public schools and the old universities to produce community feeling provides further reinforcement for the suggestion.

Furthermore, the de-schoolers certainly have a point when they draw attention to the common habit of thinking of education in terms of years spent in a recognized institution. The United States grade school system was the original target for this criticism, but it may be applied with some force to English conditions. Compulsory school attendance was only introduced in this country just over a hundred years ago, and since that time the period of compulsory attendance has been progressively extended from six to eleven years, and educationalists appear to be agreed that this should be regarded as definitely a minimum, as many pupils as possible being encouraged to remain longer. In both of the last two major Education Acts, of 1918 and 1944, provision was made for part-time attendance at colleges for early leavers, and although neither scheme survived the economic climate, they illustrate the legislators' belief in the efficacy of institutional education. Increasingly, access to the more desirable jobs is governed by possession of formal educational qualifications. More and more training takes place in formal educational institutions rather than 'on the job', and even part-time courses are progressively more college-based than works-based, sandwich courses and block release being preferred to day release. The period of training steadily lengthens over the whole range of occupations, none illustrating the process better than teaching itself. And it is not only officialdom which thinks in these terms. One of the most interesting educational phenomena of the past hundred years has been the periodical rise, from among the consumers themselves, of a demand for the period of education to be extended. Repeated attempts, from the time of the higher grade schools through to the 1960s, to draw a distinction between 'secondary' and 'higher elementary' education have been thwarted by the desire of pupils, encouraged by their parents, to remain longer at school. Since 1945, the same phenomenon has appeared in higher education. De-schoolers would probably want to argue that here is evidence to support their claim that schooling destroys the capacity of its alumni to manage without institutional help.

The de-schoolers can also find support in the marked hostility shown by many professional educators and administrators towards educational self-help. Teaching has become professionalized; teachers in state schools must be certificated, and the unions have not taken kindly to suggestions that ancillaries be used in schools. It is very difficult indeed for parents to gain permission to educate their children at home; those who have attempted to do so have encountered discouragement at the very least from local education authorities. Few teachers, it would seem, are very interested in active co-operation with the home. Parent-teachers' associations generally end up as fund raising agencies, or merely organize a few social or cultural activities. Conscious of the sociologists' revelations about the effect of social class on educational opportunity, teachers are, if anything, increasingly inclined to view their work as a crusade against the influence of the family.

The tendency is always towards greater organization, even of those areas previously left to self-help and commercial enterprise. One such territory, very little cultivated hitherto by institutional education, is that of the part-time student working at home, whether for specific vocational certificates, for general qualifying examinations, such as GCE, or for external degrees. Such students have had virtually no official assistance, unless they could find a technical college nearby which offered a relevant course. They either worked quite independently or signed on with commercial correspondence colleges. These establishments made it their function to provide what the customer wanted. They were often prepared to offer advice on courses, if asked, but by and large, if the customer wished to follow a curious and apparently useless combination of courses, that was his affair, and the courses could be provided. Correspondence courses are the classic example in education of private enterprise meeting a public demand. From the professional educator's point of view they have many of the faults of the early nineteenth-century private school, which arose to fill an institutional vacuum in a very similar way. Their drop-out rate is enormous. Students often follow courses which are ludicrously narrow or heterogeneous. Quality of tuition varies widely and unpredictably.

The institutional vacuum is now being filled. Technical colleges and evening institutes offer a progressively wider cover. Examination authorities and professional bodies increasingly stipulate that courses shall cover a spread of subjects. The Open University has appeared with programmed courses, tutorial meetings, residential courses, advisory services, and all the rest of the apparatus of organized education. Above all, while allowing a wide range of selection to the student, it introduces that *bête noire* of the de-schoolers, the requirement that students studying one subject must complement their course with certain other subjects. Of course the Open University may be right to do this. We are not obliged to accept wholly and without criticism the de-schoolers' strictures upon planned curricula. But it remains clearly true that the old days of private enterprise and student initiative are going. Even part-time students for higher degrees, who at one time were chiefly inclined to complain of the impossibility of obtaining information and assistance from the university to which they were nominally attached, now find themselves in a far more structured situation, often faced by examinations, or the necessity of producing course work or periodical reports of progress achieved. The whole postgraduate superstructure of higher education has become more closely integrated with the rest of university work. Far more postgraduate work is now done on a full-time basis, and we have already noticed how often postgraduate students appear as leaders of student opinion.

So the relationship which Illich suggests to lie between urban industrial societies, universal formal schooling, and the growth of autonomous stages of childhood and youth has some points in its favour. But when one examines the evidence with a critical eye, some awkward facts emerge to suggest that the case is not quite so simple as it appears. For example, while it is certainly true that problems specific to childhood and youth have emerged with particular force in the twentieth century, and that they are most apparent in industrial nations, they are not peculiar to such societies. Classical Athens, urban perhaps, but assuredly not industrial, was much troubled by the dissidence of youth. Socrates was put to death because his teachings were thought to undermine established authority among the young, and Plato spent much effort in devising a detailed system of education. It was based upon a concept of education as a preparation for adulthood, but it stipulated a long course, even by modern standards, and it advocated the segregation of childhood and youth in age-specific institutions. Even in the less urbanized society of pre-industrial England, wealthy families were inclined to delay their children's graduation to adulthood. Indeed it was one of the symbols of high status to do so, and the age at which a child completed his full-time education was governed far more by his social class than by any other criterion, a fact well known, for example, to nineteenth-century educationalists when they recommended secondary education with different leaving ages for children of various social positions. Children of these families showed all the characteristics of modern rebellious youth. A glance at eighteenth-century boarding schools suggests that pupils of that period had very little to learn from their modern descendants in the arts of persecuting either their teachers or each other. Their antics attracted less attention because they were relatively few in number. They enjoyed the privilege of the wealthy of being expected to sow their wild oats and they enjoyed, outside the classroom, an independence unknown to the modern child. In addition there was no national press or television to make their performances fashionable. It does not seem to be the case that childhood and youth in their modern connotations are inventions of industrial society, but rather that in such a society, conditions which previously affected only a small and select minority are extended to the population at large.

Neither is it true that childhood and youth as autonomous stages are necessarily associated with compulsory formal education. After all Rousseau was the great advocate of the autonomy of childhood, and he was no supporter of formal education, or of schooling in any form. We have seen that one of the immediate results of his teaching was a revival of domestic education, and it is difficult to find anyone among his followers who was prepared to advocate schooling except as a last resort. Twentieth-century progressives have followed his teaching in this respect. Their schools have generally been outside the state system, and frequently small, with much emphasis upon personal relationships and very little on formal organization. They have taken hardly any account of official qualifications or certificates, either for teachers or pupils, and have consistently stressed self-expression and self-learning. And yet these are the people with the most to say about intrinsic value of childhood; the phrase 'child-centred' was coined to describe their approach. They are very difficult to fit into the de-schoolers argument.

Again, while we have seen reasons for agreeing that length of school or college life carried great weight as a measure of educational success, it is not, in European educational systems at any rate, the only criterion. In fact, success in examinations is much more important, at least in the job market, and attendance at school or college, however long unless accompanied by relevant certificates of examination success, has little sales value. Until very recently it was rather difficult for pupils to remain at school after the legal leaving age, even if they wanted to, unless they were at least nominally working towards an examination. It is probably true to say that in colleges and universities the unsuccessful student finds it even more difficult than hitherto to keep his place. Obviously this reliance upon examinations as criteria of educational achievement is open to criticism, but not to the criticism that its advocates confuse attendance with education. This would only be a valid argument if satisfactory attendance guaranteed success in examination, and although there is some substance in such an allegation in respect of colleges of education, any university student or pupil faced by 'O' levels has reason to know that it cannot be upheld in other fields.

But, most significantly from the point of view of this study, the de-schoolers' case simply assumes the existence of age-specific, obligatory and monopolistic school systems, and, as we have noted in chapter 1, these are very recent developments, in a mature form more recent than the cultures of childhood and youth whose existence they are supposed to explain. It would not be difficult simply to reverse the case we have been examining, and argue that school systems arose in response to the problems thrown up by the appearance of childhood, perhaps relating this to the effect of mechanization and factory legislation upon child employment. But to do this would merely be to attempt to score debating points. The weakness of both cases lies in their search for a single effective cause. The relationship between education and social change is always complex, and it is difficult to determine whether social change was caused by the educational system or whether the educational system was the consequence of social change. In our particular case the interaction between education and other social phenomena is especially complicated, and it will be as well to attempt to disentangle one strand at a time.

Chapter 3

Technological development and educational expansion

A start may be made by looking more closely at the connection between technological change and educational expansion because, although we may have reservations about accepting too simple an account of their relationship, it is clear that some relationship does exist. It is certainly true that since the Second World War the great public interest in education has been due, more than anything else, to the belief that in a new age of science and technology, education—and by this is always implied formal schooling—is a critical investment both for individuals and for society. This belief has been expressed by educationalists and politicians of all countries and all political persuasions, and has become, as the de-schoolers correctly point out, an orthodoxy. So we have Jean Floud writing (Halsey, Floud and Anderson, 1961, p.1):

> Education is a crucial type of investment for the exploitation of modern technology. This fact underlies recent educational development in all the modern industrial societies. Despite tradition, in every case the development of education bears the stamp of a dominant pattern imposed by the new and often conflicting pressures of technological and economic change.

In the same book P. F. Drucker writes (p.15):

> An abundant and increasing supply of highly educated people has become the absolute pre-requisite of social and economic development in our world. It is rapidly becoming a condition of national survival . . . a developed society and economy are less than fully effective if anyone is educated to less than the limit of his potential.

A committee appointed by the National Union of Teachers reached the same verdict in the early 1960s, although giving a slightly different slant to its argument (National Union of Teachers, 1962, p.1):

> There are many proposals for giving more education to our people . . . they must be carried out quickly—both to enable individuals to become better citizens, more capable of meeting the challenge of life in an increasingly complex society, and because our economy will increasingly fall behind those of our rivals if we do not make a big and continuing effort to train our men and women. Britain is not rich in oil or minerals, but it is rich in talent. We believe our national survival depends wholly on the manner in which we use our human resources.

A few years previously Sir Winston Churchill presented the motive of economic nationalism in an even blunter form (*The Times,* 6 December 1955):

> In the last ten years the Soviet higher technical education for mechanical engineering has been developed both in numbers and in quality to an extent which far exceeds anything which we have achieved. This is a matter which needs the immediate attention of Her Majesty's Government . . . if we are—not to keep abreast—but to maintain our proportionate place in the world.

As Sir Winston Churchill implied, Britain was not the only country in which investment in education was regarded as a means of preserving or expanding national power. In a message to Congress in 1963 President Kennedy observed that (Hutchins, 1970, p.16):

> This nation is committed to greater advancement in economic growth, and recent research has shown that one of the most beneficial of all such investments is education, accounting for some 40% of the nation's growth and productivity in recent years. In the new age of science and space improved education is essential to give meaning to our national purpose and power. It requires skilled manpower and brainpower to match the power of totalitarian discipline. It requires a scientific effort which demonstrates the superiority of freedom.

Vaisey and Debeauvais quote the Italian minister of education as remarking that (Halsey, Floud and Anderson, 1961, p.40) 'Education in itself is a fundamental economic fact . . . the highest productivity is in the human capital'. The expansion and improvement of educational facilities have been considered to be of prime importance for the emergent nations, and the extent and length of public schooling has frequently been used as an index of progress or backwardness. The heyday of the economic motive for educational expansion was the 1950s and early 1960s. More recently, economists and educationalists have been more cautious in claiming educational development as a cause of economic progress, pointing out that countries at different stages of economic growth may make different demands upon the educational system, and that it may be necessary to exercise selection as to who is educated, what they are taught, and to what standard. There is, perhaps, a clearer realization that personal investment and public investment in education might have different and even conflicting motives. But these qualifications have not yet made much impression outside specialist circles, and it is probably fair to say that most of those who think about the question at all, would support the notion that educational expansion was in itself a national as well as a personal investment.

Of course, although this has been a dominant theme in educational thinking since 1945 it is not exclusively a post-war phenomenon. From the middle of the nineteenth century, industry and government were being warned of the danger of foreign competition to our industrial supremacy, and many commentators recommended increased and organized educational provision as one of the most necessary reforms. For a number of converging reasons the 1850s and 1860s produced an outbreak of public interest in education. The massive industrial and commercial lead established by Britain in the early nineteenth century was seriously challenged for the first time. The Great Exhibition of 1851 was a triumph for British products, but even then influential voices were heard warning that certain foreign countries were making faster progress than Britain. By the time of the Paris Exhibition of 1867 the relative decline of British industry was too obvious to be avoided, and J. P. Kay-Shuttleworth was only one of numerous writers who drew attention to the advantage enjoyed by continental countries in their more efficient educational systems (1969, p.6):

the more thorough primary instruction of such countries as
Prussia, and the opportunities afforded to their artizans for that
superior education which leads to a knowledge of the technical

relations of science and the arts, afford to foreign workmen advantages which ours must have in order to maintain a successful competition.

At the same time the country became aware that its military as well as its economic position was threatened. British armies performed badly in the Crimea between 1854 and 1856 and in the Indian Mutiny of 1857, raising disturbing questions about the quality and training of officers and men. In contrast the Prussian forces displayed formidable strength and efficiency against the Austrians and French, and again this efficiency was attributed in large part to the superior Prussian education system. The practical consequences of public concern about education were not unimportant. The Science and Art Department was founded in 1853 to encourage technical education, and three years later the Committee of Privy Council on Education was reorganized as the Education Department. Public expenditure on elementary education rose very sharply. The annual grant for 1851 was £151,000; by 1859 it was £837,000. A series of committees of enquiry—the Newcastle, Clarendon and Taunton Commissions—investigated elementary and secondary education. Perhaps most importantly in the long run, numerous attempts to bring elementary education under some form of public control culminated in Forster's Act of 1870, and Forster was quite explicit in recommending his bill on the grounds of economic necessity (Hansard, 17 February 1870):

> We must not delay. Upon the speedy provision of elementary education depends our industrial prosperity. It is no use trying to give technical teaching to our artizans without elementary education . . . . If we are to hold our position among men of our own race or among the nations of the world we must make up the smallness of our numbers by increasing the intellectual force of the individual.

Since the 1860s economic nationalism has continued to inspire pleas for educational expansion, and from time to time public opinion has been peculiarly responsive to such pleas. The turn of the nineteenth and twentieth centuries produced a panic about foreign competition comparable to that of the 1850s and 1860s but even more intensive. Prussia—by this time Germany—and France remained the most immediate and obvious threats, but the appearance of the United States as a major industrial power aroused particular concern, producing a newspaper scare in 1900 and 1901, which involved papers as different as *The Times*, the *Daily Express* and the *Daily Mail*.

As in the 1860s, various groups found that their interests coincided in demanding a more comprehensive educational system, groups which, on the face of it, were unlikely allies—business men, imperialists, scientists, socialists, liberals. The common ground between these apparently conflicting groups was national efficiency. They took up and developed Forster's idea that a relatively small country without the massive resources of manpower and material available to some of its competitors, must make the most efficient possible use of its supplies of intelligence and expertise if it wished to remain in competition. In order to do this, they argued, the country must develop its educational system. Secondary, technical and higher education must be expanded to produce the necessary supply of administrators, officers, scientists and technologists. Elementary education had two functions: to produce a literate, intelligent and responsible work force, and—a point which received special attention at this time—to widen the pool of selection for advanced education so that no talent was wasted. Sidney Webb described the schools of the London School Board, with which he was associated, as 'a vast capacity-catching machine'(1904, Chapters I, II, III *passim*). Men of very different political persuasions used strikingly similar language to refer to the necessity for educational and other social reforms. Lord Rosebery, the Liberal prime minister observed that (Semmel, 1960, p.62):

> An Empire such as ours requires for its first condition an
> imperial race, a race vigorous and industrious and intrepid . . .
> in the rookeries and slums which still survive, an imperial
> race cannot be reared.

His remarks were almost exactly echoed by Sidney Webb (1906):

> How, even, can we get an efficient army—out of the stunted,
> anaemic, demoralized denizens of the slum tenements of our
> great cities? . . . It is in the classrooms . . . that the future
> battles of the Empire for commercial prosperity are being
> already lost.

The Webbs formed a group known as the 'Co-efficients' to consider the improvement of national efficiency. It included a remarkable membership of distinguished contemporaries—Edward Grey.

Bertrand Russell, H. G. Wells, Julian Corbett, Henry Newbolt, L. S. Amery, Alfred Milner, Bernard Shaw and R. B. Haldane. Haldane wrote a series of books—*Education and Empire*, 1902, *Universities and National Life*, 1911, and *National Education*, 1913— in which he drove home the point that (1902, p.86) 'What we need is the recognition that in this problem of education lies our future; that on it depends our position as the leading commercial nation of the world'.

Another similarity with the 1860s was that fear of military weakness reinforced concern about industrial decline, and it is often difficult to disentangle the strands of economic and political nationalism. Quite frequently writers urged educational reform for economic reasons in military terms, or made a direct comparison between economic and military campaigns, as did T. H. Huxley in 1887 (*The Times*, 21 March 1887):

> We are entering, indeed we have already entered, upon the most serious struggle for existence to which this country was ever committed. The latter years of the century promise to see us in an industrial war of far more serious importance than the military wars of its opening years.

Many would not have wished to make too clear a distinction between the requirements of economic and military efficiency, regarding them as complementary aspects of national power. Milner, Rosebery and Haldane would certainly come into this category. But through the 1890s it is possible to trace an increasing emphasis upon military strength, rising to an almost hysterical burst of jingoism at the time of the Boer War, when Britain's political isolation and military inadequacy were unmistakably revealed.

Again the practical consequences of public enthusiasm for education were very substantial. The Board of Education Act of 1899 and Balfour's Act of 1902 mark a major advance in government participation in educational administration and policy making and, for the first time, the country had a recognizable national education system. A beginning was made in opening secondary and higher education to talent, in liberalizing the elementary school curriculum, and in making provision for the education of handicapped children. Progress was made in the welfare field, and important legislation was passed, not directly educational but in the same area, concerning child employment and juvenile offenders.

So far we have discussed the demands of technological society upon education as a unitary factor, but any serious examination makes it obvious that the situation is really far more complicated than this. Although numerous writers, business men and politicians agree upon the necessity of educational expansion their motives and aims are very different, and if we are to understand the rise of formal schooling to its present position of virtual monopoly we must attempt to disentangle the most important of these.

From our standpoint of the 1970s we naturally think first of specific instruction in science and technology. We have become accustomed to measuring the efficiency of educational systems largely in terms of their production of skilled manpower, so much so, that it is regarded as a serious malfunction of the higher education sector if it produces large numbers of arts and social science graduates with no specific outlet for their skills. This outlook is not novel. Kay-Shuttleworth, Huxley and the 'Co-efficients' were entirely in sympathy with it, and the repeated derogatory comparisons between English universities and their German and American counterparts in the late nineteenth and early twentieth centuries drew much of their ammunition from the inadequate vocational preparation offered by English institutions. The demand for vocational training is very relevant to this study because it was nearly always, at least in the nineteenth and twentieth centuries, a demand for formal instruction. In an important sense even apprenticeship had been 'formal' in that instruction was deliberate and fundamental to the process, but in the nineteenth century apprenticeship was of very little significance except as a means of entry to some of the more prestigious professions, and when Playfair, Huxley and Magnus spoke of technical education they were thinking of regular courses of instruction in specifically educational institutions. The shift away from 'on the job' training has accelerated through the twentieth century.

The expansion of formal vocational training has been so prominent a feature of the educational scene in the last twenty years that we may be dazzled by it, and thus exaggerate the historical importance of the demand for trained manpower for educational expansion in England. Certainly it had very little to do with the beginnings of mass elementary education in the last quarter of the eighteenth century, because no real demand for technical training arose before the 1840s at the very earliest. The early industrial revolution was not a period of great technical innovation nor of the extensive application of science to industry. Technical progress came chiefly from the discoveries of self-taught inventors who rarely had any systematic scientific knowledge, and from the intensive use of unskilled and semi-skilled labour.

In the 1830s and 1840s there was a sporadic discussion of technical education, and even some attempt to provide it. The Mechanics' Institutes frequently had ambitious plans for classes in the hope of improving the efficiency of the working population, and of widening the pool from which new inventors might be drawn. Thus one contemporary writer urged (Claxton, 1844, p.101):

> I want every workshop in the country to be filled with experimenters, and especially with men, who, from reading and thinking, shall have learned how experimenting may be done with advantage. If such were the case—if it were as much so as it easily might be—who can doubt that an incredible multitude and variety of inventions and improvements in the arts would spring up in every direction.

But this was wishful thinking. Such classes enjoyed little support either from workmen or from manufacturers, and were very rarely an important part of an institute's work, which was chiefly recreational. Schools of Design, which were founded in many of the major industrial towns in the 1840s in consequence of a scare about the quality of British industrial design, had the same experience. Many foundered, and those which eventually flourished did so chiefly by cutting their direct links with industry and concentrating upon non-vocational work.

It was in the second half of the nineteenth century and particularly after 1870, that the need for technical education really began to attract public attention. In large part this was due to foreign economic and political competition as we have previously seen, and there was ample room for concern on this score. Between 1870 and 1913 British industrial output more than doubled, but the world output increased four times. In 1870 Britain produced one-third of the whole world output of manufactured goods; by 1913 the proportion had shrunk to one-seventh. Britain was no longer even the leading industrial nation; it was overtaken by the United States in the 1880s and by Germany shortly after 1900 (see Ashworth, 1960, p.34). But industrial changes were also important. The period from 1870 to 1914 was the great age of the mechanization of industry, and therefore, of the application of science and technology (Ashworth, 1960, p.31):

> The trend of change is well illustrated by the difference between the untheoretical, common-sense approach which led Bessemer to his cheap method of making steel, and the careful marshalling of scientific knowledge for the solution of a specific problem which twenty years later enabled Gilchrist Thomas to devise the basic process of producing steel from phosphoric ores.

But even then, although there was much talk about industry's need for trained men, and of the greater efficiency of Continental and American educational systems in meeting this need, surprisingly little of a practical nature was achieved. Workmen showed little interest in the courses offered by whatever technical institutions existed, while manufacturers did not send their employees to colleges and evening classes, and attached little importance to the possession of formal qualifications in making appointments. Only in commerce was there any large demand for trained workers, as clerks, book-keepers etc., a demand which had to be met for many years by importing foreigners, especially Germans, as office workers. One feature in the commercial field of considerable consequence for the future was that office work, previously a male preserve, was being taken over by women. In 1891 8 per cent of clerks were women; by 1911 the proportion was 32 per cent.

No significant improvement occurred in the supply of or demand for technical education before the First World War and, if anything, there was a contraction after 1902 in the provision (see Argles, 1964, p.62). In the session of 1909-10 only 4,000 full-time and 4,000 part-time day students were registered in all the technical colleges in the country. Three years later, 1,487 full-time engineering and technology students were enrolled in English universities and 1,199 advanced full-time students at technical institutes. This compared with 11,000 similar students in German technical high schools.

A complex of factors combined to produce this indifference to technical training and of these, sheer complacency was perhaps the most important. Although commentators with experience of United States and Continental industry continually attempted to arouse the country to the increasing threat to its economic position, they were curiously unsuccessful. British business men and their employees had become accustomed to economic supremacy, and found it difficult to appreciate the seriousness of the challenge offered by countries which they were used to classifying as 'underdeveloped'. This does not argue any unusual obtuseness on their part; public opinion is generally slow to comprehend the significance of revolutionary changes, particularly when their effects are relatively slow and cumulative. Professor Barraclough has suggested, for example, that although the political, social and intellectual systems of the nineteenth century had broken down irretrievably by the early 1900s, and although there was a general awareness that circumstances were changing in a fairly dramatic way, the implications of these changes, and in particular their political effect upon European nations, did not achieve any popular acceptance until the 1960s (see Barraclough, 1967, pp.16ff). So it need not cause any surprise that nineteenth-century business men were inclined to dismiss the critics as Jeremiahs, and to regard British economic pre-eminence as something pre-ordained and unalterable.

But even if they accepted the reality of the foreign challenge, they did not necessarily see technical training as a solution to their problems. With the exception of a very few who had been educated on the Continent, they had not themselves received any formal technical training, and they were by no means convinced of its value. As self-taught men they were very dubious of the effectiveness of such training in practical skills which, they thought, had to be acquired on the job. Their views on this matter were reinforced by a deeply ingrained suspicion that carefully guarded industrial secrets might escape if trainees from different firms were brought together for classes. As a rule, the only technical training which they were prepared to countenance was instruction in the scientific principles underlying their crafts. Thus, a witness before the Royal Commission on Technical Instruction of 1872 remarked (Cotgrove, 1958, p.34):

> If you mean by technical education attempting to teach a man his business by a college course, I think it is a very mischievous delusion indeed; but if you mean that, in addition to his practical training, you would give him some theoretical training . . . I think that would be very useful.

This attitude, as it happened, coincided with a long-standing English prejudice against practical instruction at all levels, with the result that, as S. F. Cotgrove remarks, 'For all practical purposes, then, technical education in the nineteenth century meant the teaching of science'(1958, p.36). Certainly the classes supported by the Science and Art Department were framed to this kind of thinking and covered such subjects as geometry, building construction, pure mathematics, machine construction and drawing, theoretical and applied mechanics, geology, physiology, zoology, steam, physical geography, magnetism and electricity, acoustics etc.

Here we have one of the reasons for the failure of these classes to interest working men. For very different reasons educationalists and employers objected to formal training in craft skills; but this was precisely what working men wanted in order to increase their earning power. Unless they were unusually ambitious or intellectually curious they found courses in geology or acoustics altogether too theoretical and, to use the favourite current term, irrelevant. In addition, they were likely to find them incomprehensible, for they assumed a fairly substantial elementary education which very few working men had the money or opportunity to acquire. Contemporary critics had no hesitation in pointing to this factor as the prime cause of the repeated failure of classes for working men. A speaker of 1850 observed that (*Nottingham Journal*, 29 November 1850):

> Mechanics' Institutions had entirely failed as such owing to the want of elementary instruction among working men. He had seen many cases in which grown up persons had come to these institutions, attempted to pick up a little knowledge, grown disgusted at the drugery of elementary learning, and had given up in despair.

Thirty years later the collapse of university extension classes explained in the same way (Wood, 1953, p.14):

> The fact was that the workers, ill-equipped with only the most scanty elementary education, had not the background or knowledge to follow the courses or to profit by them . . . . One workman is reported to have said 'I'm all in a fog like—I don't know where I am and I don't know what he's talking about.'

And even if a workman acquired the elementary education necessary to follow and benefit from the courses he was offered, the conditions under which he lived made prolonged study a burden which only the most resolute could sustain (Harrison, 1961, p.13):

> Under the best of health which they enjoy, they are subject to feelings of langour and weariness which people do not feel who

live in healthy situations and breathe pure air when they are asleep. This feeling is forced off by necessity on the six days of labour; but on Sunday, when this is not the case, it is felt perhaps more than at any other time, giving them a disinclination to exert their mental or their physical powers.

Even if we accept that the demand for instruction in science and technology was surprisingly slight in the nineteenth century, we might reasonably expect to find a dramatic expansion in the twentieth century. But again we would be disappointed. Certainly there was much talk about the need for trained manpower. Britain's relative economic position continued to decline and the two world wars emphasized the inescapable connection between industrial development and national power. Both wars produced waves of government concern about the low level of investment in industrial education and research, and the whole period was punctuated by official reports on the subject. But until after 1956 rather little resulted from all the committees and discussions. Some progress was made. Technical colleges increased in numbers and, rather hesitantly, in size. The National Certificate scheme was introduced immediately after the First World War, originally in mechanical engineering and chemistry, and new subjects—electrical engineering, naval architecture, building, textiles, commerce—were added from time to time, although, even by 1939, the scheme covered only a small sector of industry. The increasing demand for qualifications at the technician level and below, led to the formation of the East Midlands Educational Union in 1911 and the Northern Counties Technical Examinations Council in 1921. At the university level the position hardly changed at all before the Second World War. Michael Argles sums the situation up by writing that (1964, p.74): 'Between 1922 and 1939 science and technology in the universities made almost imperceptible progress, and in the case of technology numbers actually declined considerably by 1928.' This was clearly related to industry's lack of interest in research, which repeatedly attracted the adverse comments of investigators. In 1916, for example, the Committee of Privy Council on Industrial Research spoke bitterly in its Report about the consequences of pre-war neglect (pp.7,8):

> We were making less than a couple of dozen kinds of optical glasses out of over 100 made by our enemies. We could hardly make a tithe of the various dyestuffs needed for our textile

industries with an annual output of over £250 million a year. We were dependent upon Germany for magnetos, for countless drugs and pharmaceutical preparations, even for the tungsten used by our great steelmakers.

Ten years later the Balfour Committee on Industry and Trade found that even the shock of war had not produced any radical improvement (Cotgrove, 1958, p.82):

> It is when we come to consider the relations between the research associations and the industries themselves, and the extent to which these industries avail themselves, in practice, of the results of research by their own associations, that we find most cause for disquietude . . . it is the imperfect receptivity towards scientific ideas on the part of British industry which is at bottom the main obstacle to advance.

In fact it was not until after 1945 that British industry even began to take industrial research seriously and to recruit staff accordingly. An investigation by the Federation of British Industries of 107 firms showed an increase between 1945 and 1950 of 213 per cent in expenditure upon research, and a later enquiry showed an increase of 32 per cent in comparable expenditure by the chemical industry between 1948 and 1952 (see Cotgrove, 1958, p.84). As might be expected there was a corresponding rise in the number of scientists and technologists employed by industry—by 82 per cent in the case of engineers, and 25 per cent of chemists between 1945 and 1950 (see Cotgrove, 1958, p.86). Even then the frequently predicted explosion of technical education was delayed. The number of degrees and diplomas awarded annually in technology actually declined slightly in the early 1950s, and it was not until the White Paper of 1956, with its suggestions for establishing Colleges of Advanced Technology, that higher education for industry really got up steam. According to that paper Britain was producing at that time 56 graduates in engineering and applied science per million of the population. By comparison the United States was producing 136 per million, USSR 280, France 70, West Germany 86, Switzerland 82. Since then as we know, technical education has expanded with immense rapidity at all levels, with an ever-increasing emphasis upon more or less continuous attendance at places of formal instruction.

All this is very difficult to explain in a satisfactory way, since most of the obvious explanations—unemployment in the 1920s and 1930s wartime dislocation, the collapse of traditionally important industries—fail to make clear why Britain's experience should be different from that of other countries. Fortunately we are not required in this study to attempt such an explanation; what is important for us, is that any attempt to attribute educational expansion in any direct way to a demand for technically trained manpower must break down in the case of Britain. In spite of repeated calls extending over more than a century by educationalists, politicians, industrialists and journalists for a more extensive system of formal technical education, it is only in the last twenty years that any really massive effort has been made in this field. This is not to say that educational expansion has been unrelated to economic development and the social changes springing from it. What it does imply is that we shall have to look for a more complex and less direct relationship.

Far more important historically than the call for specific technical training, was a demand for general education preparatory to vocational training on the job. This was of great consequence to the expansion of formal education at all levels—elementary, secondary and higher—and at all levels the requirements were essentially the same. First, it should provide a background of academic competence, the necessary level varying very widely with the profession which a particular child was to follow. Second, the work should serve to develop the child's general intelligence. The Victorians were strong believers in the transfer of training, and took the view that school work, especially if difficult and intrinsically unattractive, served as a powerful mental exercise, strengthening the mind as physical exercise strengthens the body. Finally, and in most people's view most important, education should provide children with attitudes which made them efficient and acceptable in their particular employment. Clearly there were wide variations in the attitudes thought proper to different children. Qualities of leadership and initiative were to be developed in potential statesmen, officers and entrepreneurs; integrity and attention to detail in managers, accountants etc; loyalty and obedience in those destined for 'followership'. The aims of preparatory education were not always drawn up quite so neatly as this, but there was in the nineteenth century a very clearly understood stratification of school provision based upon the type of career pupils were likely to follow, a stratification which continued to have much influence upon the organization of secondary education in the twentieth century, and also upon the relationship between elementary and secondary education, There was also a quite explicit recognition that the 'hidden curriculum', the system of routines and expectations governing roles and relationships within a school, was at least as important in the formation of a pupil's character as the formal content of lessons.

It will be necessary to look at the preparatory function of elementary education in a wider context in chapter 5. Here it is enough to point out that on two occasions the role of the elementary school in feeding industry was particularly obvious. At the turn of the eighteenth and nineteenth centuries one of the great attractions of the monitorial schools was that they provided exactly the training in obedience and routine conscientiousness which was required for children who were to enter the labour-intensive warehouses and factories characteristic of that stage of the industrial revolution. As the advertisement for one school declared, their motto was 'cleanliness, subordination and order', and these qualities were much in demand by contemporary employers. A hundred years later, employers wanted rather more from their recruits. As we have seen, this was the age of the mechanization of industry, and accordingly of an increasing demand for pupils with a reasonable degree of literacy and numeracy and a less restricted intelligence, who could be trained as clerks, foremen and engineers. It is for this reason that we find business men and industrialists giving enthusiastic support to higher grade schools, and to the widening of the curriculum in the senior standards of elementary schools, although as prominent ratepayers we might expect them to resist such expensive schemes in the interests of economy.

In this chapter we are chiefly interested in the preparatory aspect of secondary and higher education. Growth in this sector was extremely rapid in the nineteenth century, deriving its impetus from one of the great Victorian inventions—professionalism. Until the end of the eighteenth century it is fair to say that there was no notion of professionalism in management or administration, public or private, nor was there any developed concept of the 'expert' in those fields which are now the preserve of the consultant—engineering, architecture, medicine etc. The professions were limited to those very few 'learned professions', distinguished less by expertise than by possession of a university degree. Activities now assumed without question to be the monopoly of experts, were happy hunting grounds for non-specialists who often established reputations in several distinct fields; one thinks immediately of the architects Wren and Vanbrugh as obvious examples. The nineteenth century produced a number of innovations together amounting to a revolution. One was the specialist with a professional training and, increasingly, with his skill guaranteed by membership of a professional association. Medicine was among the earlier professions to organize itself in this way, and was unusual in that legislation played an important part in the process. The Apothecaries Act was passed in 1815, introducing the registration of practitioners, and the Medical Registration Act appeared in 1858. The British Medical Association was established in 1856. Other groups whose conduct was controlled by legislation were ships' officers and mine managers. Numerous professional associations were founded—that of civil engineers in 1818, the Law Society in 1825, veterinary surgeons in 1844, mechanical engineers in 1847, architects in 1848, naval architects in 1860, gas engineers in 1866, surveyors in 1868, chemists in 1877, accountants in 1880, to name only a selection.

Another innovation, clearly allied to the first, was the notion that such specialists required training. In most cases in the nineteenth century, this was acquired through apprenticeship which flourished at this level after it had almost died as a method of learning a craft. One effect of the Apothecaries Act was the establishment of medical schools in many large provincial towns, in which intending practitioners could supplement their apprentice training. Very slowly and hesitantly the same notion spread to the military sphere. A few naval and military colleges were established during the Napoleonic Wars, but until 1857 they were really boys' schools. Then, under the pressure of revelations about English incompetence in the Crimean War, the entry age was raised to between sixteen and nineteen, and a competitive examination for entry was introduced, although with certain limitations in the case of Sandhurst, where, candidates had to be nominated by the Commander-in-Chief. The East India Company also had its own college, at which Malthus was one of the first professors, but nothing comparable was provided for the home civil service. Nevertheless, the rapid expansion of the civil service, especially after 1830, its opening to entry by competitive examination from the 1850s, and a tradition of professional competence associated particularly with Edwin Chadwick and some of the inspectors, were major factors in increasing the demand for secondary education, especially as it was accompanied by the appearance of an entirely new breed of municipal administrators.

A feature of the invention of professionalism which is especially significant for us here is that it was associated with a drive to widen the pool of selection. In part this was a product of a conscious move towards a more democratic organization of society. The standard method of appointment and preferment had always been nepotism, and no one had seen any need to apologize for this. Rather the reverse, in fact, for it was taken to be a primary duty of any man of position to look after his dependents in the distribution of offices. The nineteenth century produced two virtually new ideas which entirely undermined the institution of 'sponsored mobility'. First, it was argued that selection on this method was unfair and that opportunities for preferment should be made much more widely available. Second, and this was almost equally novel, selection should be based on merit, the best man for the job being appointed regardless of his connections, or lack of them. In the early part of the century these arguments were generally advanced on grounds of equity, deriving from the kind of democratic sentiment we associate with the French Revolution. The Benthamites, however, arrived at similar recommendations, basing their case on the greater efficiency to be gained by rational means of selection from the largest possible catchment area. As the century passed and nationalist and collectivist trends became stronger (see below, chapter 5) so the argument from efficiency gained strength, while the argument from equity was also reinforced as the suffrage was extended and the pool of candidates with an adequate preparatory education expanded.

Whatever the grounds for advocating a move towards 'contest mobility', there always emerged a prescription for an expansion of secondary and higher education, and this was reinforced by two other factors. Education had always been regarded as a profitable investment, and long before the nineteenth century gifted young men of no particular family had been able to improve their social position by acquiring an education which qualified them for preferment in the Church or elsewhere. A popular form of charity had been the endowment of scholarships to help such pupils through grammar school or university. With increasing social mobility, and particularly with the nineteenth-century stress upon selection by public examination, education became an even more attractive investment. The other factor was closely related to this, and it concerned the qualifications for gentility. Until the nineteenth century it had been fairly clearly understood, that one was, or was not, a gentlemen according to one's birth. In England it was, in fact, possible for wealth to buy gentility, but not as a rule in one generation. Normally, it was the son or grandson of a nabob or industrialist who achieved full acceptance into county society. But this situation had become very confused, and a sign of the confusion was the existence of several different, and not wholly compatible, sets of criteria for determining gentility, For example, there was a vague, but persistent, notion that moral conduct or delicacy of sentiment might be set against birth or possession of a landed estate. In the confusion one test of gentility which achieved increasing currency was that of education (Clark, 1962, p.255): 'it came to be increasingly assumed that a gentleman would have the education of a gentleman.'

An increased demand for secondary and higher education did not necessarily imply an increased demand for schooling. It was perfectly possible for such an education to be given at home, either by tutors and governesses, or by parents if they had the time and knowledge. In fact, a surprisingly large number of children, by modern standards, were educated at home, and under the influence of Rousseau and his followers, the number increased in the late eighteenth century. Even up to the end of the nineteenth century, domestic education remained important among the middle and upper classes. The census of 1851 estimated that as many children were privately educated as attended all the public, proprietorial, and grammar schools combined. As might be expected, significantly more girls than boys were educated at home, but both the Taunton and Bryce Commissions recorded that about 11 per cent of Oxford and Cambridge undergraduates had been privately educated. But increasingly, parents tended to send their children to school. From the mid-eighteenth century until the 1830s, the chief beneficiaries of the increased demand were private schools, which enjoyed their greatest era of prosperity before they were gradually pushed out of business by proprietory schools, the revived public schools and, at the end of the century, by the new and revived grammar schools.

We can see why domestic education gave way to schooling in this case. Education by private tutor is inevitably an expensive business if competent tutors are employed, and in a period of enlarged demand the cost of efficient tuition is likely to rise disproportionately as good tutors achieve rarity value. Furthermore, it is a demonstrably uneconomical technique, pedagogically speaking, since any individual tutor's efforts are limited to a very small group of pupils, perhaps to only one. For those reasons the popularity of private tuition is likely to fluctuate widely according to the quality of opposition offered by available schools. Only a few parents will feel the cost of private tuition is justified by its exclusiveness alone. Many more will take the opposing view, that the barriers it places between their children and others are a drawback; and these will patronize good schools where they exist, if only because of the opportunities they offer for companionship and social training. In the late eighteenth-century endowed schools, public and grammar, were at a peculiarly low level of efficiency and moral tone so that there was every reason for parents to hesitate to use them, but in the nineteenth century they were immensely improved, especially in the degree of physical and moral supervision exercised by the staff, the marginal advantages of domestic education being accordingly very much reduced.

More rapid social mobility and new attitudes towards social class reinforced the move towards schooling. We have already seen that education might be used as a criterion of status, an increasingly important criterion as the validity of other tests—birth, for example, or ownership of an estate—was challenged, because education received support from a number of otherwise hostile interests. Benthamites seeking efficient officers and administrators, democrats looking for a way of opening careers to talent, aspiring parents, and conservatives seeking to control the rate and direction of change, all looked to education as an agent in their designs and all, for different reasons, favoured schooling provided that efficient schools could be found. Benthamites wanted the most economic use of manpower, and therefore approved of large classes; the more pupils a teacher could supervise the greater return one could obtain on one's capital. Democrats preferred schooling because they saw that private tuition must inevitably be the prerogative of a minority and that only through the agency of schooling could education be made generally available. They were very conscious, too, of the disadvantages suffered by many children in their home backgrounds, and looked to education to compensate for these. Obviously, such an education had to be obtained outside the home which had proved a limiting influence on the child's development. With a rather different emphasis, ambitious parents of moderate means accepted this argument, appreciating also that by attendance at the right school their children might acquire, not only the academic qualifications for successful careers, but also useful friendships and experience in social intercourse with children of the status to which they aspired. Conservatives agreed with these parents, seeing that the deluge might be delayed, if not averted, if young men of talent before achieving promotion, could be initiated into the life style of the ruling classes by attendance at schools patronized by their children.

As promotion by education began to become a reality in the mid-nineteenth century a new consideration appeared, adding force to the case in favour of schooling against private tuition. One desired effect of the adoption of education as a criterion for appointment was to widen the pool of selection. But this introduced a new problem. With increased frequency, and especially for more desirable posts, a number of the applicants were quite unknown to the appointing board, and could not produce references from men known to the board. For success in a career, therefore, a premium was placed upon education at an institution of established reputation from which a reference would carry weight, and whose headmaster would be known, if not personally at least by virtue of his office, to prospective employers. It is no coincidence that it was at the same period that public examinations, whose sale value in the employment market could be more or less exactly assessed, began to establish themselves. And it is an indication of the way in which the field for employment continued to open out and depend upon school achievement as a measure, that by the early twentieth century public examinations had multiplied to the point at which they had to be rationalized by the introduction of the school certificate.

One of the features of early nineteenth-century secondary education which attracted most criticism was its insistence upon a narrow classical curriculum. Some of the attacks were based upon a fairly crude pragmatism, amounting to little more than a plea that vocational training should form the basis of school work. These, as we have seen, aroused rather little interest and certainly never influenced the curriculum of English secondary schools in any direct way, if we exclude a possible expansion of commercial training by 'writing schools'. More significant, then and later, were allegations that classical studies left out of account large areas of knowledge important for an understanding of modern society, notably mathemathics and the physical and biological sciences, the foundations of the contemporary industrial and intellectual revolutions. Change was delayed in the public and grammar schools, partly by a conservatism nourished by their self-perpetuating nature, partly by difficulties in amending obsolete and restricting foundation statutes, but largely by dramatic changes within the classics themselves, which in the hands of some of the more able nineteenth-century scholars became a genuine instrument of intellectual enlightenment. In a very class conscious society, too, the classics enjoyed the advantage that they were the staple of schools attended by the aristocracy, so that parents with social ambitions often wished their children to study them regardless of their vocational or educational value. Nevertheless, experiments with new subjects continued throughout the century, particularly in private schools, and by the time the Board of Education came to draw up regulations for the payment of grants to secondary schools in 1904, a standard 'modern' curriculum had appeared, based upon English, mathematics, science, modern languages, history and geography, Latin appearing as a prestigious option. This programme of studies has held the field to the present day in spite of competition from an ever-lengthening list of modern subjects, and in spite of recurrent criticism that it still fails to do justice to the paramount importance of science and technology in contemporary society, neither fitting pupils for training in these fields, nor providing those who are not intending to study them further with the conceptual apparatus necessary to comprehend the language, problems and methods of science. Pupils who leave school without such a conceptual framework, it is argued, are in the same position in a scientific society as illiterates in a literate society. They are unable to play a full part as citizens, and must leave discussion and policy making to experts, thus removing the basis upon which democracy rests.

The apparently unbridgeable gap between those with scientific training and those without, which attracted so much attention in the 1960s in the 'two cultures' controversy is not simply the result of perversity or obscurantism on the part of teachers, although it has certainly been exacerbated by the difficulty of attracting first-rate scientists into teaching. It arises partly, at least, from a long anti-specialist tradition in English education. For reasons, which are not altogether clear, the English have for long regarded the specialist with suspicion, favouring the all-rounder as likely to have a balanced, unbiased viewpoint unclouded by vested interest. Even in the nineteenth century, when the amateur began to be replaced by the professional in administration, management and to some extent even in the armed forces, specialist technical training was at a discount and the new professionals were expected to be men of wide and flexible competence, concerning themselves with policy, and making use of specialist advice on technical matters. Clearly this tradition is by no means dead today in management, for example, or the higher levels of the civil service.

As we might expect, this attitude was reflected in education where, as we have seen, greater stress was laid upon character building than upon academic excellence, except insofar as the effort involved in academic achievement was seen as contributing to development of character. Specialism in any branch of learning was distrusted as something to be deferred as long as possible, preferably until the university, and a recurrent criticism of public examinations was that they encouraged a narrowing of the curriculum; 'narrow' is a word with strongly derogatory connotations in English education. When the General School Certificate was instituted it was designed as a grouped subject examination with the precise intention of avoiding concentration upon a few subjects.

Since the Second World War the 'generalist' trend in English education has been strengthened under two pressures arising from the increasing dominance of science and technology. Although not precisely anti-scientific, or at least not necessarily so, these have combined to prevent specialization by schools in science at a time when on many grounds such specialization would seem to be rational. On the one hand it is argued that in the present period of the 'knowledge explosion' when new jobs with new skills are invented every day, an increasing proportion of people's lives is spent in training during which time they acquire esoteric knowledge which separates them from their fellows, rendering communication with specialists in other fields difficult or impossible. To counteract this divisive process, so the argument continues, training should be delayed as long as possible and education should be general, aiming at enlarging the understanding of the pupil, and his powers of communication. The objection here is to specialization of all kinds, and not only to specialization to science, and it has affected secondary, further and higher education producing, for example, the 'agreement to broaden the curriculum' and the introduction of general studies into sixth forms, wider degree courses and deferred specialization in universities, and a whole new empire of liberal studies in technical colleges.

The second line of argument is that the study of science and technology is inherently dehumanizing and needs to be balanced by the humanizing effects of literature, history, music and the arts. It is a product of this thinking that the word 'humanities' has been revived as a generic name for complementary courses, more or less equivalent to 'liberal studies'. The basis of this argument is narrower and more explicitly anti-scientific, but it tends to reinforce the demand that courses be 'broad', non-specialist and non-vocational, and to strengthen the existing bias in favour of a literary rather than a scientific basis for the curriculum.

Very similar conclusions are often reached by committed supporters of technical training. They start from the observation that at a time of very rapid technical innovation, training which is too specific may be self-defeating since it produces workers whose skills rapidly become obsolete, and who must either be expensively retrained or become unemployable, at least in a job of comparable status to the one for which they originally qualified. The solution which is urged is the substitution of education for training, by which is implied a course encouraging critical insight by the students into the processes which they are learning, so that they acquire a grasp of the principles underlying their trade. Such students, it is hoped, will be more versatile, able to use their general understanding to learn quickly any new techniques. A related argument is that the highly specific nature of much industrial work leaves the individual worker with very little appreciation of the significance of his function in the business, and that this is a source of low morale, job dissatisfaction and, in consequence, loss of production. Humanitarian arguments thus join with commercial interest in recommending a broader training, allowing a student to see the relationship between his own and related crafts, and the contribution of his skill to the whole process of production.

Our examination of the connection between technological development and educational expansion has produced rather negative results. Until very recently, specific technical training in formal educational institutions has not flourished in this country, and we certainly cannot attribute the massive expansion of formal education in the nineteenth century in any direct way to a demand for technical training, although since the middle 1950s this factor has become much more important. The rise of mass elementary education in the early nineteenth century occurred quite independently of any demand for training personnel, and although secondary schools were much influenced by the need for general education prior to vocational training, the demand for their products came far more from the professions, the armed forces, government service and commerce than from industry. However, these developments in secondary education do point the way to the next stage in the search for the origins of the schooled society, for they drew attention to the social consequences of nineteenth-century industrial developments.

Chapter 4

The social consequences of technological change

From at least Elizabethan times elementary schooling had been used as one of a group of agents of social control and social welfare, along with the workhouse, the constable, the bench of magistrates, and various charities—almshouses, hospitals, lying-in trusts etc. Throughout the seventeenth and eighteenth centuries sporadic attempts had been made to establish spinning schools, where pauper children could be taught a trade, together with the virtues of thrift and industry, thus making them useful and independent members of society at, it was hoped, little cost to the community, the profits of their labour off-setting the costs of residence and instruction. The charity schools founded in the early eighteenth century under the auspices of the Society for Promoting Christian Knowledge addressed themselves to the same problem of pauperism, but faced in addition the legacy of social disturbance from the revolutionary period in the mid-seventeenth century, and also a serious problem of defection from the Church of England in both the Dissenting and the Catholic directions. M. G. Jones makes the point that (1964, p.4):

> The political and social unrest of the seventeenth century
> contributed in no small degree to the desire of the upper and
> middle classes to establish social discipline among the poor . . .
> an organization which would provide for them religious and
> social discipline would solve two acute problems of Church and
> state, the growth of irreligion and of pauperism.

The anti-Catholic bias of the charity schools emerges in charity sermons such as that of the Archdeacon of Huntingdon who said, in 1706, that children who knew the Anglican catechism 'would never stoop to beads and Latin charms, nor bow their necks to the dark slavery of Rome' (Jones, 1964, p.35).

This use of elementary education is illuminating, because it goes at least some way towards providing the explanation we are seeking for the modern emphasis upon formal schooling. Education was being used in a missionary role, as a counterweight or corrective to dangerous tendencies in society, or to indoctrinate actually or potentially hostile sub-cultures. Pauperism, for example, was seen as a threat. Paupers made no contribution to the community, and were, indeed, a source of considerable expense to those prosperous enough to be assessed for the poor rate. Their numbers seemed to be steadily and irreversibly rising, producing a corresponding rise in the cost of relief. They were at least a potential breeding ground for unrest, and with the meagre and grudging relief allowed them the temptation to vice and crime was very strong. To many respectable people, particularly those of nonconformist opinions, poverty was in itself a moral delinquency, a sign of fecklessness, irresponsibility, and unwillingness to work—in contemporary terms, lack of 'industry'. This punitive attitude died hard—if it has died completely even now—and it dominated the administration of the poor law well into the twentieth century. The head of the Poor Law Division remarked in his evidence to the Royal Commission of 1905 that the pauper must suffer (Furth, 1956, p.155):

> first the loss of personal reputation (what is understood by the stigma of pauperism); secondly the loss of personal freedom, which is secured by detention in a workhouse, and thirdly, the loss of political freedom by suffering disfranchisement . . . the work must be both monotonous and unskilled . . . . You have got to find work which anybody can do, and which nearly everybody dislikes doing.

To combat poverty various methods were employed, with motives ranging from the philanthropic to the punitive. Experiments were made in outdoor relief; parishes were allowed to combine to establish workhouses; the law of settlement was enforced, or not, as seemed most appropriate at the moment; charities were extended, and the eighteenth-century invention of joint stock financing was used to extend the scope and efficiency of charitable organization. But education gave promise of being most effective, because by inculcating children with the virtues of industry, thrift, and responsibility, which their parents were presumed to lack, it seemed likely to act as a preventive. For this reason the provison of elementary education figured prominently in most schemes for the treatment of pauperism.

A characteristic pamphlet was published by Rev. John Acland in 1786 under the title *A Plan for Rendering the Poor Independent of Public Contributions*. It proposed compulsory contributions to national friendly societies as a form of accident and unemployment insurance and went on to recommend charity schools in terms which were to be repeated by a host of writers and speakers over the next thirty years:

> I may venture say that all idleness in children is just so much
> Vice in the bud, which will be sure to shoot forth in due
> season; and that therefore it is a matter of serious concern to
> a State to bring up children in early habits of industry, and to
> prevent as much as possible all the assemblies of young persons
> at chuckfarthing, pitch and toss-up, and the like idle
> amusements, which, when justly considered, are only so many
> nurseries for idleness, dissipation, gambling, and the gallows.

Elementary education was similarly prominent when it came to confronting the political and religious challenge offered by the Catholics and Jacobites, and the uncomfortable social doctrines left over from the Civil War period. Here there was a particular reason for the appeal to education. Adults who were disaffected for whatever reason were unlikely to be fertile grounds for missionary efforts, but it was well known that children are more susceptible to indoctrination, so that it made good sense to concentrate on them. Where the community was not disaffected it was still sensible to use education in a preventative function, inoculating the children, so to speak, against later infection.

Where education is used in this way it must take the shape of schooling, or at least of formal instruction by some agency other than the home. The whole point of this kind of indoctrination is that it is used to make up for inadequacies or to counter malignant forces in a child's existing environment. If the home, or the peer group, or the local community is providing an inadequate or an inappropriate education—'education' is used in its wider sense here— then the supplement or replacement must come from an outside agency. Founders of charity schools were quite clear about this. It might be that their motives for founding the school were entirely philanthropic; they wished to provide opportunities for the children which their parents had not enjoyed. Or it might be that they wished to keep the lower classes reconciled to their limited field of social and political action, to re-affirm what Defoe referred to as 'the great law of subordination'. In neither case could they reasonably look for the teaching to be done from within the community, although very often members of the community who had passed through the course might be sent back to spread enlightenment or quietism. The natural, and in practice, universal resource was to appeal to formal schooling.

So, by the mid-eighteenth century elementary education was well understood to be an instrument of social policy, and in particular a weapon in the struggle against poverty and its related social problems. Already, magistrates, clergymen, poor law guardians, and others in contact with local administration were conscious that these problems were growing in extent and urgency. The continual rise of the cost of relief left them in no doubt of this, and affected them very directly as major contributors to charity and to the poor rate. But in the 1790s the situation became critical, and, as J. R. Poynter remarks (1969, p.45):

> The intellectual air was thick with proposals for their relief and the overseers and gentry of almost every parish were busy with devices for keeping the poor, not only alive, but well-affected towards their superiors and the state.

Three abortive bills for poor law reform were introduced to Parliament, two in 1796 and a third in 1800; the Society for Bettering the Condition of the Poor was established in 1796 campaigning, among other things, for medical advice for the poor, prison reform, and improved treatment for children in factories; two major studies of poverty were published, F. M. Eden's *The State of the Poor* in 1797, and T. R. Malthus's *Essay on the Principle of Population* in 1798; the Speenhamland system was only one of several attempts to improve the administration of outdoor relief. Elementary education was central to all these efforts. The monitorial school was introduced, its minute supervision and ceaseless activity exactly answering the demand for training in industry and obedience, and its cheapness appealing to hard-pressed charity organizers. All the leading figures in the anti-poverty campaign stressed the importance of elementary education; several were prominent supporters of monitorial schools. Sir Thomas Bernard, of the Society for Bettering the Condition of the Poor, spoke of 'the extraordinary supposition that an uneducated and neglected boy will prove an honest and useful man', and in a pamphlet of 1809 he described how the Society was converted to the necessity of education to its plans (Poynter, 1969, p.196):

It became evident that nothing essential or permanent could be done for bettering the condition of the poor, without the improvement of their moral and religious character, by an increase of places of worship for their sacred duties, and of schools for the education of their children.

Samuel Whitbread, speaking on his poor law bill of 1807 asked for schools to be established by vestries, with free education on the rates for the children of labourers: 'In the adoption of the system of education I see the enlightened peasantry frugal, industrious, sober, orderly and contented because they are acquainted with the true views of frugality sobriety, industry and order'. Malthus wrote of opposition to education of the poor as 'illiberal' in sentiment, and 'feeble' in logic (see *The Essay on the Principle of Population*, 1798, p.526).

This surge of concern for social welfare had certain immediate causes—a series of bad harvests from the mid-1790s, producing scarcity prices and consequent unrest, and the events of 1793/4 in France which inspired an anti-Jacobin panic and eventually led to war. But far more profound and longer lived factors were operating which meant that, although interest in reform fluctuated, it never really declined, and repeatedly rose to periods of general excitement like that of the 1790s. In the second half of the eighteenth century, Britain reached the stage of economic 'take-off' and entered a period of acute social and economic difficulties associated with the industrial revolution. Briefly, the country had to shift, in a relatively short time, from a rural/agricultural economy with a small and dispersed population to an urban/industrial economy with a large population, the great majority packed into, by historical standards, massive conurbations. This involved an increasing proportion of the population, not only in geographical and vocational moves, but in a complete dislocation in their style of life. The disturbance was probably greatest for the first generation to be affected, partly because change of any kind was a greater novelty to them than to their children brought up in an atmosphere of instability, and partly because for a time the country's social institutions were unable to cope with the complexity and immensity of the problems forced upon them so that there was a period of experiment—if this does not imply too deliberate and considered a process—very expensive in human suffering. After about 1850, an urban working class culture began to emerge, and new administrative machinery was devised with the power, will and expertise to improve somewhat the quality of life in the new industrial society. But even when the first troubles of industrialization and urbanization had been negotiated there remained the question of how the young were to be trained for and initiated into the new society, a society in many ways more complex and demanding upon its members than the old.

The problem which first caught the public attention was a rising population. Between 1801 and 1851 the population of England and Wales almost exactly doubled, and if there had been no other complicating changes this increase would have been enough to place an intolerable strain upon welfare agencies in the absence of major innovations in organization and methods. But the rise in population did not simply mean that two people lived where one had lived before. The distribution as well as the size of population altered drastically, and the late eighteenth and early nineteenth centuries saw the appearance of the large industrial town, a new phenomenon and one which, especially from the 1820s, tended to obsess reformers. In such towns many thousands of working people were massed together, making it very difficult for more prosperous citizens to remain ignorant of their conditions of life. These conditions, too, were displayed in their most unattractive light. It is questionable whether the individual dwellings of urban working families were, by and large, worse than working class houses had always been, and rates of pay and prospects of betterment were generally better in urban than in rural areas. It does not do to forget that rural poverty, unemployment and unrest were causing concern long before Manchester and Birmingham began to attract attention, nor that Luddism was largely a rural movement. But the cumulative effect of square miles of urban slums, unrelieved by parks and open places for recreation, was infinitely depressing particularly, perhaps, to workers brought up in the country—the great majority at this period. And absence of sanitation, refuse disposal, street cleaning, building by-laws and police, an irritant at worst in a small village, was inevitably disastrous in a town of 50,000 or more inhabitants. Social statistics, a new invention, made it clear that death rates in towns, especially among children, were immensely high, and that they rose very significantly as one passed from the relatively salubrious middle class areas into the working class slums. Furthermore, whatever social welfare agencies existed were completely overwhelmed by the influx of new inhabitants. Many industrial towns were more or less new creations, springing up due to some accident of economic geography where only a small village had existed before. In such towns the only nominal local authority was the vestry, barely competent to manage the affairs of a parish, and wholly unable even to begin to cope with running a town especially if, as was often the case, the whole population was dependent upon a single industry so that unemployment in one works frequently meant unemployment in all.

It was not only the lack of physical amenities which was so depressing; there was another side as well. It is hard to avoid a feeling that the new industrial towns were unnecessarily squalid and unattractive, even given the circumstances of their creation. They seemed to possess no civic pride or patriotism, or even much sense of municipal identity. One feels that the inhabitants, largely raised in rural surroundings, lacked the skills and attitudes necessary for urban life, and were too numbed by their experiences to do much more than survive without making much effort to improve their surrounding. Asa Briggs has drawn attention to the deeply seated English bias in favour of rural rather than urban life, and points out that prosperous and influential citizens, who might otherwise have led a campaign for civic improvement, tended to move out of town whenever their career and financial situation made this possible. He quotes an observation of G. M. Young: 'The best society of Philadelphia was trying to improve and glorify Philadelphia; the best society of Manchester was trying to get out of it' (Briggs, 1963, pp.69-70).

Improvement came rapidly in the second half of the nineteenth century. One of the features of this period was municipal pride, not infrequently manifesting itself in competition between cities such as Leeds and Manchester in the establishment of public buildings, colleges, libraries, museums, art galleries etc. At the end of the century the rise of the red-brick universities was to be much hastened by the determination of the great provincial cities to have their own universities. At the same time, there were unmistakable signs of the growth of an urban working class culture, based upon spectator sports, the public house, music halls, brass bands, oratorios, working men's clubs, neighbourhood shops, and occasional outings to seaside resorts. Whatever its limitations in terms of high culture, this was a real advance on the raw, brutal, frontier life of fifty years earlier. But at the end of the eighteenth century all this was far in the future, and people had still to learn how to turn an encampment into a community.

Increased social and geographical mobility also caused concern. The changing geographical location of industry, together with the growth of large industrial centres with insatiable appetites for labour-encouraged working people to move further and more often than before. Changes in agricultural techniques involving less labour-intensive work added a negative incentive to the positive incentives offered by factories and warehouses. This, as was fully appreciated by contemporaries, had far-reaching effects on social control and welfare. By removing labourers from the villages in which, under the old dispensation, they would most likely have lived and died, it removed them from the conservative influence of their community and of its recognized leaders, the gentry, placing them instead in large anonymous masses of similar people where community controls and natural leaders were virtually non-existent. It is not merely coincidental that at this very time the concept of a society divided horizontally into classes began to replace that of a vertical division into 'interests'. Drawing working people together into large towns gave them an appreciation of their collective identity, of their communal grievances, and of their potential strength when acting together. Of course, it had a corresponding effect upon the middle and upper classes whose hostile and fearful reaction, exemplified in the Combination Acts and the repression of working class political movements during and after the Revolutionary and Napoleonic Wars, was instrumental in crystallizing the class system and injecting an element of hostility.

Their fear was redoubled by the French Revolution, since the French apart from setting a deplorable example in their domestic affairs, threatened to export democratic ideas, and attracted a number of admirers in this country. The French Revolution marked a watershed in class relationships, one of the most important reasons why the social problems we are discussing came to a head in the 1790s. It has been observed that even as late as the Gordon Riots of 1780, the use of the London mob was accepted as a legitimate political tactic; aristocrats were rabbled not so much as aristocrats but as representatives of an opposing 'interest' (Thompson, 1963, p.72). 'After the French Revolution no Whig politician would have risked, no City father condoned the tampering with such dangerous energies'. Once again, the hostile reaction of the upper classes had the effect of precipitating the very result that they feared, for there is little evidence of autonomous working class political consciousness in the 1790s, and none of any general disaffection. Radical movements of the day were supported chiefly by the upper and middle classes and attracted little working class interest, while the Loyalist Associations of 1792/4 were supported by all classes and suspected Jacobins and democrats were roughly handled in popular demonstrations. By the end of the Napoleonic Wars, however, political disaffection among the working class was a reality, showing itself in violent anti-establishment demonstrations in the frequent bouts of economic depressions.

While geographical mobility contributed to the appearance of horizontal stratification, increased social mobility tended to create uncertainty and confusion about status, which in turn produced a defensive attitude among those who felt their position to be challanged. Industrial and commercial developments called into being new occupational groups which had no established position in the recognized hierarchy, and which could not conveniently be equated with existing occupations, while some existing trades rose or fell very sharply in economic standing due to technical innovation— hand-loom weaving and framework knitting were cases in point. Confusion was confounded by a change in attitude towards the achievement of status, the beginning of the Victorian idealization of the self-made man. The early days of the Industrial Revolution were a period of genuine opportunity for men of originality and enterprise. Many achieved, in one generation, national or even international fame, and thousands made more modest progress starting as labourers and finishing as overseers, managers or partners. To many this was a development to applaud, and such men were models to set before aspiring boys and girls. But not everyone was so confident. Others saw the due order of society being upset. They might be prepared to accept some movement; English society had never been entirely closed to merit or wealth, but such wholesale promotion and relegation was too much, and they certainly could not approve of making social mobility into a virtue.

Fear, whether of political unrest or of loss of status and influence, was certainly a powerful force moving people towards interest in reform. Unwillingness to meet ever-rising poor rates was another. But it would be unfair and misleading to ignore the motive of pure philanthropy. People were genuinely horrified by the conditions under which the poor were obliged to live, particularly so since the industrial poor was such a new phenomenon, one which perhaps brought home to them the plight of the poor in general. They were also in a state of mind to take notice. England was passing through a moral revolution almost as complete as the industrial revolution and exactly contemporary with it. By modern standards this was an astonishingly violent and brutal age in which a staggering amount of immorality was accepted in private life, and corruption in public life. But there were clear signs of change. The Prince Regent's grossness was already becoming antiquated in his own day, and a more serious tone was spreading at all levels of society, accompanied by religious observation, respectability and an interest in good works. During the Regency, the new morality was vigorously disputed by the more old-fashioned raffishness, but it gained ground rapidly and what we generally understand by 'Victorianism' was a familiar social phenomenon long before Victoria was born. One of the effects of the moral revolution was to create a new sensitivity to suffering and injustice, so that it frequently appears that new social problems were arising when, in fact, old problems were being discovered and faced for the first time or were being approached with sympathy and a real desire for amelioration. Scandals in public administration, too, long accepted as inevitable and hardly worthy of censure, were now uncovered and attacked as higher standards of public and private conduct were demanded.

Two distinct strands may be traced in the new morality, although it was quite possible for both to exist in one individual and to reinforce each other. One we may call the 'Evangelical' strand, providing that we take care not to confine the category exclusively to those who were technically Evangelicals. This was essentially a religious movement, reacting against the eighteenth-century Broad church in which tolerance had become too often a cloak for indifference and slackness, and it emphasized the necessity for a Christian to accept the duties and responsibilities of a Christian life. These responsibilities involved caring for the spiritual and physical needs of others as well as oneself, and a strong missionary spirit was characteristic of this group. Much importance was placed upon piety, and upon setting high standards of achievement for oneself and others. Followers of this school could be humourless, self-righteous and intolerant, but they were a powerful driving force for reform, and it must be said that the eighteenth century was frequently prepared to tolerate conditions which, in all conscience, were intolerable. And if there was about the Evangelicals an ostentatious piety and an obsession with personal sin which strikes one as repulsive and hypocritical, it becomes at least understandable when we appreciate the conditions against which they had to struggle. It may be, indeed, that the nineteenth-century emphasis upon respectability was a necessary stage towards making life tolerable in an urban/industrial society.

The second strand we have already discussed in a different context in chapter 2. It may be called the 'Romantic' strand, and finds its most consistent expression in the writings of Rousseau and the poets Blake and Wordsworth, although it received important support from the eighteenth-century cult of 'sensibility'. It lacked the single-mindedness and discipline which made the Evangelical movement so potent a reforming force, but it did make two major contributions. One was its doctrine of the innocence of childhood which did much to stir sympathy for the suffering of poor children, spilling over into a more general concern for the helpless, apart from encouraging reformers by its challenge to the deeply ingrained belief that mankind was innately sinful. The other was its disenchantment with contemporary society, and particularly with industrial expansion. This could fall away into a jejune and sentimental medievalism, but it had its value as a counterweight to the crass and uncritical worship of 'progress' which frequently overlooked the personal cost of industrial development.

Advocates of social reform had their hands strengthened by two other intellectual developments. One was a new belief in the possibility of reform, deriving much of its credibility from contemporary success in science and technology. It was argued that man's new success in controlling and exploiting his physical environment indicated that social problems might be solved by similar methods. Increased prosperity lent some power to this case, as did the successful translation of joint stock methods from commerce to charity organization. But undoubtedly the strongest argument for this point of view was derived from psychology. The current psychological orthodoxy, deriving from Locke and Hartley and elaborated by French writers, notably Helvetius, carried environmentalism to its limit, asserting that a person's character was entirely the result of his experience, and denying the existence of innate dispositions. From the reformers' point of view, the most significant implication of this doctrine was that character was infinitely malleable, an optimistic conclusion since it meant that the most hardened wastrel or sinner could be redeemed by judicious social engineering. If working people were placed in tolerable surroundings with decent houses and adequate facilities for recreation, and if the necessity of thrift, honesty, sobriety and industry were brought home to them by education, then social problems would very largely be dissipated, leaving only the hard core of unavoidable hardship due to bereavement, injury to the breadwinner, old age etc, which was thought to be the proper object of charity. This optimism was reinforced by another characteristic of contemporary psychology, perhaps its greatest weakness. Too much emphasis was laid on rational thinking, and the account of motivation was quite inadequate, particularly in its neglect of the unconscious and irrational—or at least, apparently irrational, elements in human behaviour. It was too often assumed that a person would always follow what to an outside observer appeared to be his best self interest so that if, for example, the evils of drink or gambling were clearly stated, drunkards and gamblers would forthwith be reformed. The human ability to give verbal assent to a proposition without allowing one's conduct to be in any way affected by it was ignored, and reformers and educators persisted in pathetic belief, to modern eyes, in the power of factual knowledge, even if acquired by rote and without understanding, to effect reform in attitudes and habits. In the context of this study, however, the failings of the current psychology are irrelevant. What is important is that it gave powerful support for reforming movements, while encouraging reformers to place special trust in education as an agent of social engineering.

For the purposes of this discussion, we may consider the functions of elementary education in the period from 1780 to the middle of the nineteenth century under two categories—social and political discipline, and preparation for industrial work—although it will not do to dwell too much on these distinctions. Throughout the period, the conservative aspect of education was paramount. Schools were established to help in keeping the labouring classes content in their social place, in checking demands for political responsibility, and in producing docile and industrious workers. After about 1850 the emphasis changed, and the radical aspect became more important. Education was seen increasingly as an instrument of social change rather than as a means for preventing or limiting it. The initial crisis of the industrial revolution had been surmounted, and the country was groping its way towards a way of life appropriate to the new economic organization. The endemic social and political unrest of the first half of the century gave way to a generation or more of calm in which co-operation between classes seemed to offer better prospects of improvement than conflict, an impression strengthened by a rapid and widely shared rise in real wages. Threats of foreign political economic competition made national unity and the efficient use of manpower desirable. It would be too much to say that the disciplinary motive for educational expansion disappeared; it remains influential at the present day, but it certainly lost its primary —almost exclusive—importance in the relatively stable and genial social and political climate of the third quarter of the nineteenth century.

But when mass elementary education was first attempted some sixty years earlier, it was as part of a campaign to restore social and political order. The working classes, it was believed, were getting above themselves, living extravagantly—poverty was habitually blamed on spendthrift habits—seeking individual and collective betterment, and demanding a part in political discussion. The watch-word of the educational campaign was 'subordination'; the poor were to be taught the necessity of their lowly place in society, and the folly, for oneself and for the community, of attempting to change it. So we find Sarah Trimmer writing in *The Servant's Friend* in 1787:

> The design of the Charity schools is to give the children of poor people such a degree of knowledge as may enable them to learn from the Holy Scriptures their duty to God and man. For this happy advantage they are indebted to the benevolence of persons in higher stations; and they ought to be very grateful for it . . . .

while Hannah More, in her charge to a woman's friendly society, wrote (McLeish, 1969, p.88):

> We wish to recommend you to do your duty in that state of life where God has placed and called you. Every disposition to

rebellion against the higher powers would prove how little you are changed in your hearts after all we have done for you; and remember that rebellion against rulers first brought on the troubles in France.

It was by no means universally agreed that providing education for the poor was, in practice, the best way of achieving the aims of the campaign. Powerful figures argued that an educated population was calmer and less liable to be roused by agitators than an uneducated one. Adam Smith, for example, asserted (*Wealth of Nations*, Bk V, ch. 1, Art. ii) that the more the workers are instructed:

> the less liable they are to the delusions of enthusiasm and superstition, which among ignorant nations, frequently occasion the most dreadful disorders . . . . They are more disposed to examine, and more capable of seeing through the interested complaints of faction and sedition, and they are, upon that account, less apt to be misled into any wanton or unnecessary opposition to the measures of government.

Malthus, taking a rather pessimistic line reached the same conclusion—education would make 'the common people bear with patience the evils which they suffer, from being aware of the folly and inefficacy of turbulence'. Parish schools 'have the fairest chance of training up the rising generation in habits of sobriety, industry, independence and prudence (The *Essay on the Principle of Population*, 1798, Bk IV, pp.493-40). On the other hand, many believed that ignorant men were more likely to be content with a subordinate position, their minds not having been opened to the possibility of anything else, while education merely gave men ideas above their station. A writer in the *Gentleman's Magazine* of 1797 put this case in its bluntest form:

> Industry is the duty to impress on the lower classes. A little learning makes a man ambitious to rise, if he can't by fair means then he uses foul . . . . His ignorance is a balm which soothes his mind into stupidity and repose, and excludes every emotion of discontent, pride and ambition. A man of no literature will seldom attempt to form insurrections or form an idle scheme for the reformation of the State.

Some pessimists saw education, not only as disturbing the complacency of the poor, but as an actively malignant force, spreading dissatisfaction and scepticism. An example was the Bishop of Rochester who said in 1800 that (Silver, 1965, p.41):

> The Jacobins of this country are, I very much fear making a tool of Methodism . . . schools of Jacobinical rebellion and Jacobinical politics . . . schools of atheism and disloyalty abound in this country; schools in the shape and disguise of Charity schools and Sunday schools, in which the minds of the children of the very lowest orders are enlightened—that is to say taught to despise religion and the laws and all subordination.

His attribution of Jacobinical views to Methodism was peculiarly unjust, but in his remarks on the consequences of schooling he voiced a widely held opinion. One of the features of the contemporary social scene which caused conservatives most alarm was the appearance of a large class of literate working men, often with a taste for reading matter of a deliberately inflammatory nature, a phenomenon which did not encourage sceptics to accept claims for education as a conciliatory force. Many would have agreed with the character in T. L. Peacock's *Nightmare Abbey* who complained 'How can we be cheerful when we are surrounded by a reading public that is growing too wise for its betters?' This reading public first caught the public's attention in the 1790s, but it was after the Napoleonic Wars, and particularly from the 1820s onwards that a large literature of autonomous working class politics began to circulate, much of it distinctly subversive in tone. One possible response to this literature was to offer rival attractions, calculated to win the minds of working men and their families to less dangerous fields, and several attempts, not altogether unsuccessful were made to do this for example, by Chambers' *Edinburgh Journal*, founded in 1832 and selling at 1½d, and the Society for the Diffusion of Useful Knowledge's *Penny Magazine*, founded in the same year. But the circulation of these, although substantial, hardly rivalled that of the mass of less desirable material. The Inspector, H. S. Tremenheere, discovered the weekly circulation of all the periodicals in a shop in Newcastle in 1851, and returned them as (Webb, 1955, p.63): 'Nine (infidel and chartist) 1,612; one (chartist only) 600; four (hostile to present institutions and of immoral tendency) 1,656; three (religious and moral and containing useful information) 688.' Such reports were not cheering to those who feared for public order, and it was not unnatural that many preferred the course of keeping education from the people. In recommending this policy they were accepting the same interpretation of the effects of schooling as their strongest opponents, for working class leaders were insistent in advocating the extension of literacy as a step towards the achievement of political power. It was Tom Paine himself who observed in the *Rights of Man* (1792, part II, ch. V) that 'A nation under a well-regulated government should permit none to remain uninstructed. It is monarchial and aristocratical Government only that requires ignorance for its support.'

On the whole, however, most moderate and liberal opinion favoured elementary education for the labouring classes, provided hat it was strictly limited in content, strongly disciplinary in tone, and was not employed as an instrument for social levelling. Teaching reading attracted almost universal approval, especially when associated with explicit moral and religious instruction and due stress on subordination. Writing and arithmetic were more controversial, and unqualified approval of teaching all the three 'Rs' was a mark of a liberal or even radical outlook. Fear of over-educating the poor, and thus giving them ideas above their station remained one of the great obstacles to improving elementary education until well into the present century, and it appeared in some unexpected people. For example, even Kay-Shuttleworth was affected by it as he demonstrated in a letter about the training of teachers, written to his partner in the founding of the college at Battersea, E. C. Tufnell (Smith, 1923, p.123):

> From the commencement of our labours we have been attentive
> observers of the proceedings of foreign normal schools; and the
> errors into which they have fallen, by a neglect of simplicity,
> and by encouraging too high aspirations among the students,
> have been a constant warning to us to avoid similar blunders.

Over-education of teachers excited special disapproval for, not only did students frequently use their training as a qualification for non-teaching posts, but teachers whose aspirations had been raised might be expected to infect their future pupils with their own ambitions for social improvement, so defeating the purpose for which they had been trained.

The same grudging and suspicious attitude towards the acquisition of learning by working people prevailed in the field of adult education and was one powerful reason for the tepid and occasionally hostile reception given by the working class to, for example, the Mechanics' Institutes. In the 1830s and 1840s, England experienced one of its recurrent waves of enthusiasm for adult education, leading to the founding in most towns of any size of Mechanics' Institutes or similar establishments. Motives for this activity were mixed, including an early and largely abortive attempt at technical training. But in the minds of the middle class sponsors of these institutions—and most were founded upon middle class support and administered by middle class committees—fears of Chartism and related manifestations occupied an important place, and they were seen as instruments for lowering social tension by demonstrating middle class goodwill in providing the institutions; by offering counter-attractions to the clubs, coffee houses and meetings patronised by working men, often with political affiliations; and by providing opportunities for reading and instruction, again on the assumption that increased knowledge would bring moderation and acceptance of the status quo. Unfortunately the middle class subscribers, who frequently retained a controlling interest, generally refused to allow religious or political questions to be discussed and censored the libraries and reading rooms, thereby driving the more thoughtful and articulate members to rival establishments, and at the same time insulting their intelligence and judgment. At Crewe, for example, where the Railway set up a library and reading room for the staff recently moved to the new town from Liverpool, subscriptions to the Chartist *Northern Star* and another radical paper were prohibited, with the result that thirty or more members left to set up a rival concern, presumably Chartist in spirit (Chaloner, 1950, p.273). At Nottingham, the Mechanics' Institute's avoidance of controversial debates, and its refusal to purchase radical literature encouraged the growth of numerous radical libraries, discussion groups and clubs where the members could make their own rules. The committee complained of the apathy of working men towards self-improvement, but one member, more acute than most, read the situation correctly (Wardle, 1971, p.178):

> It had been said that one man could bring a horse to water but five could not make him drink. In their own instance they had found the water, but for some reason or other the operatives would not drink the water they had found them; while, on the other hand, they found 700 of them drinking other water their own way.

Closely related to the elementary school's function as an agent of social and political discipline, and in practice hardly distinguishable from it, was its task of producing from a population reared in a rural/ agricultural tradition a workforce fitted for an urban/industrial economy. Until the last third of the nineteenth century the progress of mechanization was not revolutionary, and industry was labour-intensive, demanding a very large labour force capable of performing rapidly and carefully tasks which required little technical skill. A class of highly skilled artisans was required, and the rise of this 'aristocracy of labour' was historically important, but not for this study. Until the industrial revolution most production was organized on some version of the domestic system. Few workmen enjoyed complete independence; most worked on a 'putting-out' or sub-contracting basis, which frequently meant that they received a very small proportion of the total profit on the manufactured article, often further reduced by rents paid for apparatus, hired often from the 'putter-out', who thus made a double profit. It is easy to idealize the life of workers in domestic industry. They were as much at the mercy of fluctuations of trade as any factory worker, more so in a way because, although incomes ceased during a slump, rents for machines did not and it was desperately easy in bad times to run up hopeless debts. Dependence upon the contractor for whom they worked was virtually complete, and when times were hard contractors saved money by reducing piece rates. Workers who complained received no more work. Such tactics caused bitterness and sometimes rioting, but the contractors had the whip hand. But domestic workmen did enjoy certain advantages, and the one which was perhaps prized as much as any was the freedom to work to their own timetable. Normally they worked on a weekly stint, and provided their work was ready for the bag-man when he called, it was their own business how this result was achieved. The consequence was that they were notoriously undisciplined in their work habits, taking a two or three day weekend, working day and night for the rest of the week to meet the deadline, and causing bitter hardship to their families who worked in ancillary capacities and were compelled to work to the same timetable. Under these circumstances quality control was inevitably slovenly, a condition exacerbated by the complex of sub-contracting characteristic of domestic industry and the consequent lack of effective central supervision.

This would not do for the proprietors of factories and warehouses. For large scale production to be economic, different processes within a factory had to be co-ordinated with some precision since one department could not be kept idle while another completed its work. Where steam power was used this was even more important, since wasted time involved unprofitable use of fuel. Employers needed workers whose attendance was regular, who were punctual, and who could work for long periods at a consistent speed; and these were precisely the qualities which, through long habit, the domestic workers lacked. Because they were more docile and easily trainable, more amenable to close supervision and, of course, because they worked for lower wages, many employers preferred to use women and children, a practice made possible by the simple and repetitive nature of much of the work. The employers' demands for disciplined workers were not in themselves absurd or malignant; large-scale industry simply could not function on the incurably individualist basis of the domestic workers. But, very naturally, workmen bitterly resented the loss of independence involved in factory work which was intensely unpopular, even when, as was often the case, rates of pay were substantially better than in surrounding domestic industries. Further resentment, again very natural, was caused when long established domestic industries were replaced by large-scale businesses, causing unemployment or reduced income, often among men who had enjoyed high status as skilled craftsmen.

The size and complexity of the new industrial units, too, brought new stresses. Most workmen had been used to a fairly close and direct relationship with their employer. They now found several grades—overseer, manager etc.—inserted between them and their employer, making it difficult for them to take much personal interest in the firm's affairs, while giving them a feeling that they were being spied upon, especially distasteful to people used to working at least nominally on their own account. Division of labour and the routine of operations, both necessary in the interests of productive efficiency, made much factory work boring and personally unsatisfying, a problem which worried even so early a commentator as Adam Smith, who drew attention in *The Wealth of Nations* to the danger that repetitive work would stultify the workers' mental faculties.

Here was a field of controversy in which employers met workers head on in almost complete mutual incomprehension. There was much to be said on both sides, but neither side showed any wish to hear the opposition's case or to understand their point of view.

Employers accused workers of fecklessness, indiscipline, idleness and failure to see their own and their employers' best interests. Workers accused employers of ruthlessly grinding their employees' faces, and of subordinating their interests to the requirements of machinery in the pursuit of profit. The dispute had much to do with the appearance of class consciousness and class hostility, and unfortunately another and related clash of ideals contributed to the same result.

In the early nineteenth century, as we shall see in chapter 5, the doctrine of *laissez-faire* triumphed over the older paternalism. For the workman this had a number of unpleasant implications. The long established systems for regulating wages and controlling entry to trades were deliberately allowed to decay, in spite of attempts by workers in some of the traditional crafts to have them revived in the 1790s. In 1813 and 1814 the relevant clauses of the Act of 1563 were repealed, marking the effective end of the old system. At the same time, a sustained attack was made upon the poor law, in particular upon those clauses permitting outdoor relief. The general aim of this campaign was to institute a society in which each person was an independent economic unit, and relationships between such units were purely contractual, depending upon the exchange of goods and services for money and implying no responsibility for each others' welfare beyond those written into the contract. Once again the aims of the campaign were not intrinsically unreasonable. The laws of settlement, for example, were a restraint on mobility of labour and outdoor relief, as organized at that time, did tend to depress wages and pauperize its recipients. The concern of a good landlord for his dependents was not always distinguishable from oppression, and was often officious, sometimes insulting. But refusal to protect wages, coupled with limitation of relief, could look like a calculated assault upon the interests of the labouring classes, particularly when taken in conjunction with the Combination Acts and the suppression of working class political movements. And the constant insistence upon the virtues of self-help and independence, whatever its real motives, could be reasonably construed as an attempt to rationalize the neglect of traditionally established duties, while undermining the equally long established working class tradition of mutual support.

A belief that labouring people were common losers from the industrial revolution was the prime reason for the appearance, in the years following the Napoleonic Wars, of a working class conscious of its independent identity. Leaders of the new class believed that they were victims of a conspiracy to exploit their labour while denying them political and social rights, and in view of the continual emphasis upon subordination and the danger of over-educating the poor, they must be allowed to have a point. On one matter, as we have seen, they agreed with their opponents. They firmly believed that knowledge was the key to power. Information, especially political information, must be freely available to everyone—this was the reason for their campaign against taxes on newspapers, and for the extensive and largely illegal cheap popular press—and so that everyone could profit by this knowledge, education also must be available. But this education must not be the carefully filtered, innocuous diet offered by charity schools, as John Doherty insisted in *The Poor Man's Advocate and People's Library* in February 1832 (Simon, 1960, p.220):

> Let us reject with disdain the stunted lessons which aristocratic pride would have us be grateful for, and provide for ourselves the abundant and unrestrained feast for our mental and hungry appetites. Let the huxtering owners of the misnamed Mechanics' Institutes, and the would-be rulers of mechanics' minds see that the day is gone by when the millions will be satisfied with the puny morsel of mental food which aristocratic pride and pampered cunning have been wont to deal out to them.

Not all working class leaders demanded education for the same reasons, and although they succeeded in co-operating for lengthy periods, their aims were not ultimately compatible. One school argued, somewhat on Marxist lines, that an inevitable opposition existed between the middle and working classes, and that the working class must establish its own educational institutions aiming, among other things, at countering quietist propaganda, and increasing class solidarity with a view to an ultimate seizure of power. Quite consistently, they were particularly insistent upon rejecting any educational facilities offered by the middle class. Doherty, clearly, was a member of this school. Advocates of 'moral force', on the other hand, saw better prospects in co-operation with the middle class, and hoped to produce a working class so civilized and refined by education, and so obviously responsible, that the case for denying them political power would be rendered untenable. William Lovett, the Chartist leader, was a characteristic member of this group. Both sides were greatly interested in adult education, establishing reading rooms, libraries, 'halls of science', and numerous other institutions, often in explicit opposition to Mechanics' Institutes and other ventures inspired by the middle class. Day schools were fewer and do not appear to have lasted after brief periods of enthusiasm had waned. It may be that working people felt that the need was too urgent to wait for the relatively slow process of education of the young, and looked, rather, to a crash course of adult education to effect the necessary changes of attitude. Some of the adult centres, certainly, were neither small nor short-lived. Professor Simon mentions that the Hall of Science at Camp Field cost £6,000, and the one at Liverpool £5,000. Other large halls were built at Sheffield, Huddersfield, Stockport, Halifax and Bristol, and there were many smaller halls (see Simon, 1965, p.235f.). The Operatives' Libraries in Nottingham, formed in protest against the policy of the Mechanics' Institute, had several hundred members and co-operated closely, holding an annual meeting at Operatives' Library Number One which existed until the 1890s with over eight thousand volumes (see Wardle, 1971, pp.185, 186).

The period of the industrial revolution has been discussed at length for three reasons. It is important in its own right for this study because the first attempts were made at this time to extend elementary education to the whole population, so that we may say that the schooled society began here. And it so happens that the campaign for mass elementary education makes an instructive case study; it is a paradigm example of the use of education to bring about social changes through inculcation of new attitudes, or confirmation of old ones, while the motives for the campaign were clearly expressed and commanded an unusually wide range of acceptance.

After 1850 pressures upon schools became more complicated. The demand that they should discipline and civilize the working class remained powerful. Although fear of political revolution faded after 1848, there remained a prodigious amount of crime and violence, and the forces of law and order were frighteningly weak. Even when law enforcement was possible, it was expensive, and it occurred to many that prevention of crime through education might be cheaper and more efficient, at least in the long run. The case was presented by J. D. Morell in an article in the eighth edition of the *Encyclopaedia*

Britannica, and as one of the early school inspectors he spoke from first hand knowledge:

> It (the government) is obliged to watch them, to intimidate them, to repress them, often to imprison, prosecute, and punish them; and the idea naturally presents itself whether, in such a case, it would not be wiser and better, as well as cheaper, to attempt some educational means of reformation, than to be ever engaged in a perpetually renewed struggle of force against force.

Since school attendance was not compulsory many of those children who might be considered to be most in need of civilizing did not appear, and when school boards imposed compulsion in the 1870s, many schools, especially those in urban areas, had to face a flood of new pupils who, apart from being very reluctant scholars, were at a stage of sheer barbarism which the modern English teacher never experiences. Inevitably these schools had to set themselves low levels of aspiration: for many children, the ability to concentrate upon an activity for a few minutes, or to obey a simple instruction was a long step forward, and ideas of cleanliness and co-operation had to be learned from the beginning. The board schools' success in civilizing these children was remarkable, and if their teaching methods were often pedestrian, and their discipline draconic, they may find some justification in the sheer immensity of the problems they faced. One historian puts their achievement at its very lowest when he writes (Ashworth, 1960, p.197):

> Before the end of the century it had become possible to ensure that very few children grew up in a state of complete savagery, and that almost all of them were introduced to habits of discipline and order, and to simple ideas of magnitude and meaning. Though it may have been seldom that they were taught to care or not to care, they were at least taught to sit still, a lesson not without benefit to industry and to society.

But he adds (pp. 198, 199): 'there still remained a far larger number than ever before who had discovered, many at the very simplest and some at a more advanced stage, how to learn something new and not to be scared of it, and how to stick at a task until it was done.

G. M. Young drew attention to another aspect of their work (1953, p.117): 'Those solid, large-windowed blocks . . . meant for hundreds of thousands their first glimpse of a life of cleanliness and order,

light and air.' More significant to this study than the board schools'
success is the fact that they had to face these problems at all, because
it reveals with great clarity the total failure of voluntary attendance
to solve them. The Victorians were fully aware of the lesson to be
learned from this. They had approached compulsory education
with great reluctance as something entirely opposed to some of their
most valued principles, but they had been inexorably driven to it by
accumulating evidence that many parents just did not send their
children to school and keep them there, even when the advantages
of attendance were plain. Except in some of the largest industrial
cities, the problem faced by school boards in 1870 was less one of
providing schools than of making sure that children attended, and in
the early school board years attendance officers were more important
than teachers, and were paid accordingly (see Wardle, 1970, p.36).
Attendance at inspected elementary schools in the 1860s rarely
exceeded 65 per cent of the children nominally on the roll, and it is
likely that non-inspected schools did worse than this. Even this
figure takes no account of the large number of children who were not
even on the roll of a school. The conclusion seemed inescapable that
to retain the voluntary principle involved danger to society because
of the large stratum of the population who received no social
training whatsoever, whilst perpetuating a grave injustice by denying
the means of improvement to those children whose parents would
not or could not send them to school.

Unfortunately the civilizing effect of schooling tended to be
temporary. When the control of the school was removed at the age
of eleven or twelve, pupils too often succumbed to the influence of
their environment. 'The discipline and order secured by the elementary schools was almost miraculous, but within two or three years
the well-trained schoolboy degenerated to the larrikin of the streets,
ignorant, foul-mouthed and predatory (Eager, 1953, p.365). From
the 1880s to the First World War there was great interest in youth
movements which, it was hoped, would reinforce the socializing
work of the elementary school by engaging the interests and energies
of boys and girls of above school-leaving age in activities which were
socially useful, or at least harmless, and which provided discipline
and social training. Many of the youth associations were religious in
origin, with a leaning towards muscular Christianity. Obedience,
cleanliness and physical fitness received much attention, often with
the support of quasi-military organization, involving uniforms,

bands, marching etc., and the names of the associations—Boys' Brigade, Church Lads' Brigade—underline the military atmosphere. Momentum was added to the socializing work of the elementary schools and to the efforts of youth movements by a campaign, which flourished in the 1890s and early 1900s, for direct moral instruction to be instituted in schools. This campaign resembled in some respects the agitation of a hundred years earlier for the establishment of Sunday schools and monitorial schools. It gained much of its strength from a feeling that the intellectual revolution of the nineteenth century had demolished the religious foundations of moral behaviour without finding any effective substitute. Sponsors of the movement were divided into conservative and radical wings, one wishing to return to the old beliefs, the other to replace them by moral instruction based on an ethical rather than a religious basis. But all agreed that the problem had to be solved by schools. Churches and families were failing to provide an effective moral training under the pressure of social and intellectual change, and so schools had to be called in to take over their responsibilities. It is a good example of the way in which schools were coming to be accepted as the automatic surrogate for any social institution which was functioning inadequately (Selleck, 1968, p.307):

> When the English home had not been equal to the burden of caring for its children's health or the English factory had staggered under the burden of foreign competition, the school had been called upon for help. Now, when the Church was deemed unable to play its part in moral instruction, the school was called on again.

At precisely the same time evidence of physical degeneracy, arising largely from recruitment for the Boer War, led to a very similar campaign for physical fitness and an extension of medical and welfare facilities, and again the school was used, almost without question, to take over functions long the responsibility of the parent.

A contributory factor to both the moral education campaign and interest in youth work, was the appearance in the 1890s of the 'generation gap' and a youth culture explicitly opposed to the values of adult society, part of the contemporary cult of modernity and innovation which made 'new' a word in vogue. Fear of foreign rivalry was also influential. Other countries, it was believed, and Germany was as often as not the example offered, had not succumbed to the moral decadence, the inability to distinguish right from wrong and to stand for the right which afflicted Britain, And this was a dangerous situation since (Hughes, 1901, pp.110,111):

> The real stability, permanence and power of a state is not measured by the number of its soldiers, the strength of its ironclads, not yet the depth of its exchequer, but rather by the moral strength of its citizens; by the uncompromising firmness of its manhood to the eternal principles of Justice and Truth.

The disciplinary motive has not disappeared in the twentieth century. Concern about outbreaks of juvenile delinquency was a feature of educational discussion during and after both world wars, especially the second, when evacuation and the effect of air raids not only disrupted much schooling but revealed to many people, for the first time, the conditions under which many fellow citizens lived. The Youth Service was one product of official alarm about wartime demoralization, and the Crowther, Newsom and Plowden Reports have all advocated educational expansion for the purposes of socialization. But, while education is still accepted as an agent of social engineering, the emphasis has changed from keeping the poor in their place to compensating for inadequate or hostile home backgrounds, so that children do not have their horizons limited by accidents of birth. The change may be summed up by saying that the social function of education is seen, not as limiting and negative, but as positive, liberating a person from his environment. A low estimate is usually made of the cultural value of society, and the family and peer groups are conceived as either educationally neutral or actively malignant. The duty of education is placed upon the school and typically, rather little trust is put in self-help or spontaneous local effort. Nineteenth-century liberals, especially those at the end of the century who drew on the philosophy of T. H. Green and Toynbee, were fervent believers in this line of thought. K. S. Inglis described Canon Barnett of Toynbee Hall, a distinguished but characteristic member of this school as (1963, p.164): 'one of those Liberals whose only article of dogma was the cleansing and uplifting power of education', and Barnett himself wrote (Inglis, 1963, p.164):

> The social problem is at root an educational problem . . .
> without more knowledge, power might be a useless weapon
> and money only a means of degradation . . . . The only thing

which Liberals can compel is education, because till people be educated they cannot be free or use freedom.

Much modern thinking about the social function of education is based upon the same gloomy estimate of society as an educational instrument, and the consequent necessity for rescue work to be done by schools and similar formally organized institutions. The Newsom and Plowden Reports are examples which immediately come to mind, and another very clear case is provided by Hutchinson and Young's *Educating the Intelligent*, where the assumption that schools are conducting a crusade against a non-educative society is quite explicitly made. The authors say, for example (1962, p.13):

> If a child is illiterate when he leaves school we cannot start again; he will remain illiterate for the rest of his life. If a child is innumerate when he leaves school we cannot start again; he will remain innumerate for the rest of his life. If a child is immoral when he leaves school we cannot start again; he will remain immoral for the rest of his life.

And when they come to discuss the high delinquency rate in the years following school-leaving, their prescription is for more highly structured activities, with school, parents, and youth service being drawn together into associations for their organization.

An extension of the same reasoning leads to more specific calls for the schools' services as a socializing agent. One of the principle motives for advocating comprehensive schooling has always been that such schools encourage mixing of different social classes. As the Labour Party Pamphlet *Learning to Live* of 1958, put it:

> In a comprehensive school those, who in later life will follow many different callings, join together in games, in entertainments in all that rich part of school life outside the routine of the classroom. At the very least this must be an influence for good.

A policy of deliberate social mixing completely reverses the long standing preference of English educators for segregation into a number of systems according to the social class and intended careers of the pupils, and certainly involves the imposition of a school system opposed to the wishes of many parents. It may be none the worse for this. An educational programme is not self-evidently wrong because opposed by parents, but we should notice that the fire of the de-schoolers is directed especially at the kind of reasoning that we have been examining here, and it is undoubtedly true that schools have taken upon themselves—or had thrust upon them— many functions previously within the purview of home, Church, or voluntary organizations.

Another motive for educational expansion which has continued into the twentieth century is the call for political education. Originally, as we have noticed, it was a fairly simple demand that the children of the labouring classes be so educated that they were resistant to political agitation and content with their limited social role. In this form, it was hard to distinguish from the social discipline which we have just been discussing, but after the mid-nineteenth century it underwent a rather similar development, becoming very much more complex and less negative. The concept of the political roles of different social classes was changing rapidly, inevitably involving changes in the political functions of education. From about the 1830s onwards, one finds increasing acceptance of the fact that a large measure of political power must eventually rest with the working class. In many the prospect aroused alarm; some viewed it with enthusiasm, as the coming of liberty and democracy, but all were agreed that a necessary pre-requisite of political power was an extension of elementary education. J. A. Roebuck remarked, when introducing his elementary education bill in 1833, that 'I wish the people to be enlightened, that they may use the power well which they will inevitably obtain', and Matthew Arnold expressed precisely similar sentiments in a letter to his wife, shortly after becoming a school inspector (Smith and Summerfield, 1969, Letters 1.17):

> I think I shall get interested in the schools after a little time;
> their effects on the children are so immense, and their future
> effects in civilising the next generation of the lower classes, who,
> as things are going, will have most of the political power of the
> country in their hands, may be so important.

In the 1860s, as the inevitability of some extension of the franchise became clear, so interest in elementary education increased, and the Parliamentary Reform Act of 1867 was a powerful argument for Forster in pressing his education bill through Parliament. Kay-Shuttleworth, writing in 1868, expressed the common view (1969, p.5):

The announcements of the intentions of the Government are a natural consequence of the recent great extension of electoral power among the classes supported by manual labour. The beneficial exercise of that power will be a measure of the intelligence and virtue of the classes who are most to be influenced by primary education. All are agreed that a well-ordered system of national education, reaching to the most ignorant and destitute, would be the firmest foundation on which our widely spread electoral power could rest.

But acceptance of the necessity of an enlarged franchise did not by any means imply acceptance of full political equality. Working men might be given the vote, but it was taken for granted that the actual ruling and administration would be done by very much the same people as before, with perhaps a leavening of able young men of working class origin who obtained the necessary status through the educational system. No one seems to have seriously suggested in the late nineteenth century that schools should be used for social levelling. Very much the reverse, in fact, for the social class stratification of education hardened. The public school system as we now understand it was a product of this period, and both the Taunton and Bryce Commissions had schemes for systems of secondary education stratified according to social class. The Woodard Foundation did, in fact, produce just such a system. Even the higher grade schools and post-1902 secondary schools were conceived as, among other things, devices for catching talented working class boys and girls and equipping them, not only with academic knowledge, but also with the values and attitudes necessary for promotion to the middle class. J. S. Maclure, speaking of London secondary schools, mentions (1970, p.90):

> how emphatically the social distinction between elementary and secondary school was brought home to the secondary school pupil by the relatively palatial buildings, and by the explanations of the staff who made it clear that those who attended were privileged persons. The secondary schools were seen as great engines of social mobility, and the scholarship scheme as a publicly sponsored instrument for elevating clever children from the elementary school classes.

Political education was seen as an important function of both elementary and secondary schools, but it was clearly understood that, while secondary schools trained children as leaders, elementary schools had the task of producing intelligent and efficient, but ultimately obedient, followers. And, as the passage from Maclure's book suggests, the difference in function was indicated as much in the organization, atmosphere, ethos, even buildings, of the schools as in their formal curriculum.

In the twentieth century the idea that different types of school should prepare children for different social and political roles has only slowly, and very incompletely, been replaced by the idea of the common school. But advocates of comprehension are insistent that children should not only study the same subjects, but should do so in the same school and, as many argue, without distinction according to ability, revealing by this their awareness of the power of informal aspects of a school's life in determining its pupils' levels of aspiration. Successive efforts have been made to introduce into the timetable specific lessons in 'citizenship', 'social studies', 'humanities', or whatever the current term may be. The contents of such courses vary somewhat, but the central aim is to equip prospective citizens with some knowledge of the working of the constitution and of central and local government, so that they can understand their rights and duties while, very often, it is hoped that the instruction will help pupils to develop some critical capacity to enable them to withstand propaganda—political or otherwise. Courses in citizenship attracted much support in the 1930s and 1940s when the totalitarian threat to democracy seemed especially dangerous, as the Spens Report of 1938 observed (Introduction, p.xxxvii):

> Democracy is now challenged, and the duty of citizenship in a democracy renders it essential that all should be taught to understand and to think to the best of their ability . . . . On the extent to which the youth of this country can be fitted to fulfil later their duties, and to take advantage of their opportunities as citizens of a democratic state, may well turn the whole future of democracy, and that not only in these islands.

Recently another wave of enthusiasm for similar courses under different names has arisen, connected perhaps with the contemporary breakdown of political consensus.

In examining the use of schools to inculcate social and political virtues, one is struck by a marked oscillation in emphasis between individualism and collectivism. We have already noticed that in the early nineteenth century, schools were used in a campaign to spread the gospel of individualism, competition, free enterprise and self-help, in place of the older belief in paternalism, co-operation and restricted competition. An important pedagogical discovery of the period was the use of competition and emulation among pupils as a method of controlling pupils and raising their levels of aspiration. Monitorial schools were specially noted for the use of complicated systems of rewards and punishments of a competitive kind, but one of the innovations made by Butler at Shrewsbury, which raised it to a very high level of academic repute, was the intensive use of competition, and he was widely copied. In part, this change was due simply to the increased size of schools, which made class control more difficult, while at the same time producing groups of pupils of similar age large enough to make realistic rivalry a possibility. But its rapid and universal adoption suggests that it satisfied a widely felt need, and within a very few years individual competition had become an integral part of school atmosphere.

By the end of the nineteenth century the cult of individual competition was being vigorously challenged. Undoubtedly, the most distinguished educationalist to react against what he felt to be the selfish individualism of contemporary society was the American, John Dewey, but in this country, too, schools were being urged to stress patriotism, self-sacrifice and social responsibility, and a series of booklets, published in 1910 under the title *Essays on Duty and Discipline* by an influential group, including Baden-Powell, Kipling, William Booth, Milner, and W. T. Stead, criticised 'the prevalent idea that mere individual freedom, unchecked and unguarded, is the one goal of life, and the only true road to self-development' (Selleck, 1968, p.303). The collective overtones to this movement could be very strong, and could carry a marked nationalist and militarist bias. Michael Sadler remarked that (Selleck, 1968, p.299):

It has often been urged by persons anxious for our social ideals that national education should be so planned, directed and enforced, as to establish and maintain throughout the whole body of the people one high national purpose, and to blend all individual wills in one common aim.

Not everyone went as far as this, but it is noticeable that education at all levels was much affected by the team spirit. The most obvious manifestations of this were to be seen in the public schools, where an almost doctrinaire *laissez-faire* outlook by the teachers towards the out-of-class activities of the boys was replaced in the last third of the century by far closer supervision, the dominance of the house system and a positive obsession with team games. Many of these character-istics were adopted, somewhat incongruously on occasion, by the new secondary schools of the early twentieth century, while the team spirit was also a conspicuous feature of youth movements, notably the Scouts.

During the 1920s and 1930s bitter experience of the consequences of an alliance of collectivism with nationalism produced a reaction, and we find writers such as Percy Nunn, recommending a return to concentration upon individual values in an attempt to avoid in England the mass indoctrination which they saw occurring in Germany and the USSR. We have seen previously how explicit political training was recommended by other educationalists for the purpose of inserting a defence against indoctrination. Other writers again, Karl Mannheim and Fred Clarke being the most distinguished, suggested that in defence against totalitarianism, it might be neces-sary to use methods of indoctrination ourselves. In the 1950s and 1960s individualism   seemed to command the support of most educators, but recently signs of a reaction have appeared. The Schools Council has been busy with 'humanities' courses, looking very like 'citizenship' or 'social studies' courses warmed over, and both in schools and the youth service we find much stress on community work, intended to divert the energies and interests of young people into socially useful channels, while making them aware of social problems. On this point there appears to be a *rapprochement* between official education and the alternative society, where communal life and the avoidance of competition and emulation figure largely.

Here is a clue to the solution of a question which clearly puzzles the de-schoolers and produces an awkward gap in their argument. A point upon which they all lay much emphasis is that schools drill their pupils into conformity. Everett Reimer writes (1971, p.18): 'School domesticates—socially emasculates—both girls and boys by a process much more pervasive than mere selection by sex. School requires conformity for survival and thus shapes its students to conform to the norms for survival.' and Illich adds (1971, p.34): 'schools select for each successive level those who have, at earlier stages in the game, proved themselves good risks for the established order.' And yet they also wish to maintain that revolt is to be found particularly among pupils and students. Reimer's *School is Dead* and Paul Goodman's *Compulsory Miseducation* both begin with paragraphs about drop-outs and the collapse of the school system. Illich writes (1971, p.34): 'since 1968 it (the university) has visibly lost standing among its believers. Students refuse to prepare for war, pollution and the perpetuation of injustice. Teachers assist them in their challenge.' At the end of this chapter I shall suggest that, for England at least, statements about mass drop-out from schools need to be treated with some reserve, but even if we accept for the sake of argument, that schools and universities are filled with rebels against the established order, we shall want to ask how this situation came about, and the de-schoolers hardly face up to this question at all. School, we are told 'has become the universal church of a technological society, incorporating and transmitting its ideology, shaping men's minds to accept this ideology, and conferring social status in proportion to its acceptance' (Reimer, 1971, p.19), and since it has a 'monopoly of both the resources for learning and the investiture of social roles' (Illich, 1971, p.34) it argues a stupefying degree of incompetence on their part to produce a rebellious generation. But incompetence is not what the schools are accused of. They are teaching not only the wrong things, but they are teaching them too well, so well, that the only hope is to disestablish them and provide alternative methods of education; society must be de-schooled (Reimer, 1971, p.19):

> Their monopoly of education has been achieved as one aspect
> of the monopoly of technology. The main reason we need
> alternatives to schools is because they close the door to
> humanity's escape from this monopoly. They ensure that those
> who inherit influence in a world dominated by technology will
> be those who profit by this domination, and, even worse, those
> who have been rendered incapable of questioning it. Not only
> the leaders but their followers are shaped by the school game
> to play the game of competitive consumption . . . . Whether the
> rules are fair or the game worth playing is beside the point.

Nevertheless the de-schoolers are surely quite correct in detecting some correlation between education and rebellion. While it would be foolish to think too much in terms of cause and effect, it is an obvious fact that expansion of elementary education in the nineteenth century went along with the transfer of political power to the working class. Those who argued that the spread of education would lead to political quietism were confounded, while those who feared, or hoped, that education would act as an irritant were proved right. At a higher academic level, students on the continent of Europe have always considered themselves, and been considered by others, as leaders in the defence of liberal and radical values against totalitarian governments of whatever type. A socially and politically conscious intelligentsia has never quite taken root in this country, but there were signs in the 1930s and again in the 1960s that it might yet do so, while radicalism within the Labour movement has received most support from the intellectual rather than the trade union wing. Even in the USSR and Eastern Europe, where pressure for conformity is as heavy as anywhere, what little unrest there has been has found a focus among intellectuals. The de-schoolers themselves are examples of intellectuals revolting against not only their own education, but also the whole structure of the society in which they live. Education does seem to have the—often unintended—result of disturbing the learner's complacency, sometimes in fields well removed from the formal content of his course.

In English schools this is due, partly at least, to the fact that the values and attitudes which they attempt to propagate in their pupils very rarely, in spite of what the de-schoolers tell us, reflect the received values of society, if by this we mean those values which would top a popularity poll. More often they are engaged in a conscious crusade against the dominant culture, trying to correct or replace what they believe to be undesirable tendencies. They must, of course, derive their aims from some pressure group; they could hardly continue to function if their work had no popular support whatever. But a diagram illustrating the social and political teaching of English schools over the last two centuries, would show them frequently shifting their position to counteract what were considered to be dangerous or unhealthy movements in popular thinking. The criticism levelled at English schools is very rarely that they reinforce uncritically the dominant culture, but on the contrary that the ethos they represent is 'antiquated', 'unrealistic', 'irrelevant' etc, which may frequently be translated as meaning that the values of the school clash with those of commerce, politics and popular entertainment. If this criticism is valid, and it is certainly true as we have suggested in the last few pages, that schools have frequently set themselves against received values, then we can see why education and revolt are related. A child will almost certainly find himself at the point of conflict between several more or less opposed cultures, his family, his peer group—and a clash here is very likely—the mass media, the school. Such tension may be uncomfortable. It is less taxing, mentally and emotionally, if one only ever hears one side of a question. But it is the beginning of the kind of uncertainty which can lead to productive questioning. It can also lead to a flight to authority, a refusal to think for oneself, and this is indeed one of the most conspicuous characteristics of contemporary youth culture, but this in itself suggests, as many commentators have noted, that the problem for today's young people is less one of exposure to overwhelming indoctrination than of an embarrassment of choice.

When we think of schooling in this way, as a counterweight rather than a reinforcement to dominant tendencies within society, we can also see why it must replace, or at least supplement, home, work and peer group as educational agencies. An educational system based upon the model of the father-to-son or master-to-apprentice relationship will almost inevitably be conservative in tendency, consisting as it does essentially of the passing on of accumulated experience from one generation to another. Where technological change is slow, or where there is a firm socio-political consensus, such a system may be adequate, particularly where the number of apprentices to be trained is limited. But where technical innovation is rapid, apprenticeship becomes a brake on progress, turning out craftsmen whose skills are obsolete, and whose training has been too narrow and too lacking in the stimulus of controversy for them to have developed the capacity to change, or even to question established ways. Similarly, where social change is desired it is futile to leave socialization to the family or peer group, the custodians of the very values which are under attack. One does not have to go outside the teaching profession to find examples to illustrate the point. The pupil-teacher system was abandoned because it was believed that it led to excessive in-breeding, a teacher's experience being limited to elementary school, pupil-teacher centre—perhaps, but not necessarily, training college—then back to elementary school. Furthermore, the actual teaching experience gained by pupil-teachers was confined to one school and this was thought, with justification, to be likely to cramp intending teachers by encouraging excessive limitation at an impressionable age. In more recent years one of the criticisms levelled at colleges of education is that their interests are too exclusively pedagogical to provide students with a really 'liberal' education, and a recurrent suggestion, based on similar reasoning, is that student teachers should have some experience of 'real life' in other fields before entering the profession.

But we must beware of supposing that education is always something imposed upon an unwilling public. De-schoolers are impressed, obsessed is perhaps the better word, with the drop-out from school, and in this country the Newsom Report, for example, made much of the failure of school to catch the interest of many less able pupils. One does not wish to belittle this problem, but it is in order to remind ourselves that reluctance to attend school and disinterest in its activities are not new phenomena peculiar to advanced technological societies. Until well into this century it was taken quite for granted by all except a few progressive educators that children would find school unpleasant, and would avoid it whenever possible. To many, the moral effort required to overcome the natural aversion to school was its principal virtue. Again, there is a danger of writing the history of education, especially of elementary education, as if schooling were always provided by the ruling classes for the enlightenment or indoctrination of the poor, whose response was, at best, dutiful but unenthusiastic attendance, and at worst, resentment and hostility. Hostility there certainly was, to an extent quite unknown today. But there was also an intense eagerness for education, sufficient to overcome the most formidable obstacles, as the biographies of numerous Victorian worthies demonstrate. And the hostility declined remarkably quickly; within a generation of the introduction of compulsory education it had been confined to a few blackboard jungles, and even in these the life of a teacher had become significantly less adventurous, and more rewarding.

There are really two phenomena to consider here. On the one hand was the characteristically Victorian emphasis on self-help. We have considered elementary education as a means of spreading political quietism among the working class and, conversely, as a means of raising the political status of the working class. But for most working people, the attraction of schooling lay less in its effect on social class and more in its possibilities for individual advancement. It is true that until the second half of the nineteenth century the demand for technically qualified labour was not massive, but for the relatively few who did acquire technical qualifications prospects were very favourable. As mechanization got under way the market for such men expanded, and the late nineteenth century was a good time, by historical standards, for the skilled workmen. Throughout the period there was a large and expanding demand for clerks, book-keepers, storemen etc., who commanded relatively good pay and white collar status, while opportunities for the ambitious man to strike out on his own were good. Literacy and numeracy were essential minimum requirements for boys who wished to rise into, or retain their father's place in, the aristocracy of labour, and until the 1880s numerous private schools flourished by providing the necessary tuition. These schools occupied an intermediate position between the relatively expensive academies concentrating upon secondary education for the middle classes, and cheap 'common day' or 'dame' schools offering baby-sitting facilities with some rudimentary instruction for the poor. In the seventeenth and eighteenth centuries they were generally known as 'writing schools', and although the term fell out of use, it serves to draw attention to the commercial bias characteristic of many of them. Most of them ran evening classes, a practice which suggests that many of their pupils were working youths attempting to improve their career prospects. National and British schools were cheaper, and if a parent was prepared to keep his children in attendance for three or four years they could obtain a comparable education. Some British schools charged higher fees than the average and catered for a social class rather above the run of elementary schools, with correspondingly enlarged curricula, while in most towns of any size were public schools, endowed or otherwise, existing particularly to provide higher elementary schooling, often with a specifically business orientation. It was a source of frequent criticism that the pupil-teacher system was used as a means of obtaining quasi-secondary education in preparation for clerical jobs. When board schools arrived they soon dominated this kind of work, especially where higher grade schools were established.

The second phenomenon, on the other hand, is the insistent demand by those who have been educated to one level to be allowed to proceed to the next. By the end of the 1870s, school boards were faced with the problem of large numbers of children who, having passed through all the standards, wished to continue at school. Higher grade schools were the logical result, blurring the boundaries between elementary and secondary education. The 1902 Act re-defined these boundaries, but within ten years they were in doubt once more, and again the reason was pressure from within elementary schools for longer and more advanced courses. Since the Second World War the school leaving age has become increasingly irrelevant, and increased demand for higher education has become a major political, as well as an educational and administrative, problem. Up to a point, these developments may reasonably be attributed to the search for improved prospects, but there are other factors at work. The Crowther Report (1959) pointed out the very marked regularity with which parents who had received a long education insisted on the same, or more, for their children:

> parents who have had more than the minimum education rarely allow their children to do with less than they themselves had. Only 8% of the fathers who had themselves stayed at school after 14 allowed their sons and daughters to leave as soon as they were legally free to do so; no less than 40% of them kept their children at school until the age of 18.

A glance at the enrolment figures for higher education reveals that the most saleable courses, from a career point of view, are by no means the best subscribed. It is the social sciences which attract students, although prospects of finding a career in which social science qualifications can be directly used, are poor. The suggestion occurs to one, and it is reinforced by contact with the students themselves, that many enrol for these courses less from the motives of personal advancement than in the hope of gaining an understanding of society and of their own role within it and, very often, of finding a standpoint from which to mount a criticism of existing institutions. In this they resemble very closely the Victorian working men, whose reading very often extended deeply into politics and theology. These were the men who resented so bitterly the censorship of their reading by Mechanics' Institutes, which often drove them into more radical courses than they might otherwise have followed.

We have discussed various features of urban industrial society which led to demands for extension of schooling, but there remain two further features which, while they did not themselves increase the demand for education, made it possible for this demand to be met. The first of these was the vastly increased prosperity which went with technological development. Professor Perkin has written (1969, p.134) that:

A general rise in the living standards, by a multiple rather than a fraction, is . . . one of the defining characteristics of an industrial revolution. Of that rise in England, in the long term and for the great majority of the population, there can be no doubt. Real national income per head quadrupled during the nineteenth century.

The effect of such a massive and rapid rise in real income is naturally to lift a large number of families well above the level of merely marginal existence so that consumer expenditure rises dramatically, and a particular rise occurs in expenditure on goods and services which may be classed as desirable but not absolutely essential to survival. Among the services which thus come within the financial reach of a much enlarged market is education. The precise impact of rising income in the nineteenth century is in dispute, but it seems to be agreed that the middle and upper working classes enjoyed very substantial improvements in their standards of living, and it is here, as one might expect, that demand for education was most active. Poorer working people, on the whole, benefited less, but even among them poverty was, in good times, a little less desperate, and the loss of earnings involved in keeping a child at school a little less critical. W. W. Rostow (1960) has argued that although Britain reached economic maturity in the mid-nineteenth century it was not until the 1930s that the stage of high mass consumption was reached, and the history of education supports this view since, although personal investment in education certainly increased enormously in the nineteenth century, it remained a minority interest until the 1930s or even later, and only in the 1960s did 'secondary education for all' begin to be interpreted in its obvious meaning.

One reason for the immense increase in popular demand for extended education is the degree to which the direct cost has been removed from the parents, and this is a reflection of increased national prosperity. The eighteenth-century state was quite unable to support anything approaching the staggering cost of a modern state educational system, and even in the 1860s an annual outlay of one million pounds in a government grant was cause for concern. Victorians had very different views from ourselves on the respective responsibilities of parents and government, a matter which must be considered in the next chapter, but even given complete acceptance by nineteenth-century statesmen of twentieth-century collectivism, there were clear limitations to what governments could afford, and a full state educational system was as much out of the question for Britain in the 1850s as is a space programme in the 1970s. Only in the twentieth century were even advanced industrial states able to mobilize sufficient funds for the establishment of welfare states.

Affluence could have indirect effects on demand for education. In chapter 3 the nineteenth-century invention of professionalism was mentioned. This was a far-reaching innovation, producing new standards of efficiency in central and local administration and military affairs, and the appearance of an entirely new social class of professional men. One important underlying reason for this was prosperity. Governments were able to offer, and—a complete innovation —actually pay, salaries sufficient to attract men of ability and to use them in responsible positions. The middle class, as one aspect of their improved standard of living, required the services of more professional men. And the new professionalism was an important source of increased demand for secondary education, and consequently for preparatory education as well.

At the same time as individual and national prosperity made it possible for more children to be sent to school and to be kept there longer, so technical innovation made the labour of children and young persons less necessary to the economy. This was not a consequence of the early stages of the industrial revolution. Quite the contrary, in fact, for the new industries of the early nineteenth century demanded large numbers of workers for simple repetitive jobs commanding a low wage, and children were ideal for this purpose. As was mentioned in a different context, their docility and teachability also made them attractive to employers faced with adult workers resentful of factory discipline. It was frequently observed that women and children predominated among factory workers and parents were accused of exploiting their children's labour, although in the admitted scarcity of work for adult men, it is hard to see what else they could do. In the second half of the century, however, rapid mechanization began to limit the jobs available to children and, together with the improved economic position of working people, this made sending children to school a more attractive proposition than before, if only because it kept them out of mischief during the day. Factory legislation may have been influential here too, but one can easily overestimate the effect of legislation on children's employment. Until the late 1860s Factory Acts were very limited in their application, and the Children's Employment Commission of 1862 makes it very clear that they were largely ignored even where they nominally applied. Undoubtedly the most effective legislation on children's employment was the institution of compulsory school attendance, which established authorities with the duty and power to see that children were not employed at all, at least on a full-time basis. It seems likely, however, that the success of the campaign against child employment in the 1860s and 1870s was due to the fact that in large scale industry child labour was becoming obsolete, and the advantages to be gained by employers in opposing or evading such legislation had disappeared. In the twentieth century the continual rise in the age at which children leave school has been made possible by a combination of individual and national affluence with the declining need for young workers.

It is possible for the employment situation to have a more positive influence on educational demand. At a time of high unemployment, it may be an attractive proposition to remove half a million or so young people from the labour market by raising the school-leaving age, or at least to attempt some less dramatic amelioration by encouraging children to remain at school. The precise effect of variations in employment is hard to predict, as most of the relevant arguments are double-edged. On the one hand, pupils may be more willing to stay at school if the alternative is unemployment. But, on the other, where unemployment among highly trained men is extensive as was the case, for example, in the 1930s, the inducement to make the effort necessary to acquire such training is much reduced. In general, however, the fact remains that opportunity for extended education for working class children, whether taken up or not, can only be available when the economy reaches the stage where child labour is unnecessary.

Chapter 5

The growth of collectivism

When we speak of an educational system we may have one of two concepts in mind. We may be thinking in administrative terms, of schools and colleges subject to central organization and control, with licensed teachers and curricula centrally determined. In this sense of the word, France and Australia are nearer to the paradigm than is England, while the USA, with weak central authority but powerful local control, is a special case. Or we may be thinking more in terms of the individual pupil, visualizing him pass through a succession of schools in an understood order, from primary to secondary to tertiary, or whatever the current terms may be. If we adopt this point of view, England has two distinct systems, state and independent, with different ages of transfer from primary to secondary. Clearly there is no reason why both forms of system should not co-exist; indeed in most modern industrial states this is the case, but there is equally no reason why one should not exist without the other, so that the independent system in this country exists without any central direction. But, however one interprets the term, education in eighteenth-century England was conspicuously lacking in system, and it is relevant to this study to enquire how it came about that systematization, in both senses of the word, proceeded with accumulating velocity throughout the nineteenth and twentieth centuries.

In the late eighteenth century two assumptions were accepted virtually without question: first, that education was the responsibility of the individual and, second, that it should reflect the recipients' social standing. State intervention in education was hardly even an open question. Writers and politicians either opposed it strongly on principle, as did Godwin and Mill, or ignored the matter altogether. Several thinkers, Adam Smith, Whitbread and Brougham for example, considered the possibility of the parish as the administrative unit for elementary education, but any more centralized organi-

zation was scouted. Even charitable provision of elementary education was embarked upon with certain reservations, as threatening
the independence and cohesion of the family, while upsetting social
order by providing for recipients of charity an education unavailable
to those members of the 'deserving poor' who retained their
independence. It had to be defended on the double grounds of an
acute breakdown of social control, and of the incompetence of many
families to provide for their children, both well established reasons
for breaking the normal rule of non-interference. For those families
who could afford to send their children to school, provision was
stratified on well understood social grounds, a rough but fairly
reliable index of social standing being the age at which one completed full time education, a criterion for educational planning
which was to reappear at frequent intervals throughout the nineteenth century.

It is usual to speak of the individualism of this period as *laissez-
faire* and to think of it as a distinct political philosophy of non-
interference in the interests of economic expansion, and it is true
that such a philosophy was developed at the turn of the eighteenth
and nineteenth century with results which are discussed elsewhere.
But the rapid acceptance of this philosophy was due in large part to
the way it fitted with, and provided a rationalization for, a much
older and much more diffuse suspicion of powerful central government, a suspicion equally strong in all classes and all political and
religious parties. Tories derived from Burke and Blackstone a belief
that power should reside in the magistracy, largely representative of
the landed interest and the parish. They stood for the paternal
powers and responsibilities of the Established Church and the
squirearchy, and feared that a strong government would interfere
with these, especially if it indulged in social legislation. Another
pillar of their doctrine was the right of property, extending to a
father's right to treat his children as he thought proper, and here
was another reason for opposing social legislation which almost
inevitably infringed somebody's property rights, as was the case,
for example, with the Factory Acts. For similar reasons they objected
to interference with endowments, corporations and trusts, thereby
making reform of endowed schools very difficult. The Tories'
attitude was not strictly one of *laissez-faire* at all since it allowed for
extensive control by landed gentry over tenants and for reciprocal
obligations upon the gentry, and Tory paternalism had to be

discredited by a vigorous propaganda campaign before *laissez-faire*, properly speaking, could be established. But paternalism of this kind allowed no place for a powerful authority above that of the parish or squire, and it thus contributed to a state of opinion in which *laissez-faire* could flourish. A central feature of the Tory philosophy was the belief that relief of poverty should be principally a matter of individual charity with the poor law to deal with what was assumed would be a hard core of long term pauperism. Charity was seen as a moral duty incumbent upon property—the complement of the deference due to the gentry from the lower orders. If poor relief became a state business, it was feared that the necessity for the exercise of this obligation might disappear, opening the way to the establishment of an irresponsible ruling class. At the same time, it was appreciated that a state system of relief, in the conditions of the time, was most unlikely to be comprehensive, and there was concern that the intervention of the government might cause private charity to dry up, leaving a vacuum in which cases of real need might go unrelieved. Indiscriminate relief was also regarded with suspicion in case it pauperized the recipients.

The Whigs were the particular custodians of *laissez-faire* in its stricter sense, being much influenced by the political economists. Their argument, in essence, was that in the conditions of an absolutely free market the most efficient industries and individual firms would survive, and that, in the long run, this Darwinian conflict would work out to the national advantage by eliminating inefficiency. Government intervention in economic matters was deprecated since it interfered with the operation of the impersonal economic laws and, by protecting inefficiency, prevented the work of weeding-out. Intervention, whether by governments or by any other associations such as trade unions, was not only undesirable but futile since, it was argued, economic laws were inexorable and inescapable. As Cobden remarked, about trade unions (Bullock and Shock, 1956, p.xxiv):

> They might as well attempt to regulate the tides by force, or change the course of the seasons, or subvert any of the other laws of nature—for the wages of labour depend upon laws as unerring, and as much above our coercive power as any other operations of nature.

In this matter, political economists were supported by the powerful

Nonconformist wing of the Whig party, although from very different premises. Nonconformists, with long memories of earlier oppression, feared that government action must always work out to the benefit of the Establishment. The rise of the Oxford Movement in the 1830s and 1840s strengthened this attitude by raising the old bogey of popery and, naturally, opposition to state power was especially marked in the field of education, where opportunities for political and religious indoctrination were so good. Edward Baines, editor of the *Leeds Mercury* and a great Nonconformist spokesman of the mid-nineteenth century 'approached as near as any man of property would allow to the position of philosophical anarchy' (Roberts, 1960, p.69), and one can catch the impassioned hostility of Nonconformist writers to government intervention from Rev. A. Wells, on proposals for state elementary education (1847, p.66):

> State power in religion, state power in education, state power in
> inspectors, state power in Whitehall, reaching over England,
> are all, as Kindred influences against Dissent, against Liberty,
> against national spirit.

Radicals shared the Nonconformists' fear that government action must always be biased and oppressive, although in their case the bias they feared was political rather than religious. They particularly criticized any enlargement in the staff of government departments, arguing that government employees might be spies or holders of sinecures. Their suspicion of sinecures was an example of the belief, accepted without question in circles far wider than the Radical party, that government officers were, as a matter of course, inefficient and corrupt. This belief, hardly disturbed before the 1840s, was a great obstacle to social reform, and as so often with such beliefs, it was largely self-confirming. While government officers were paid badly and often grossly in arrears, capable men were unlikely to be recruited, and temptations to corruption were strong. Such men as were recruited were unlikely to take a critical line against the powers which appointed them. And while the civil service was comically understaffed inefficiency was inevitable, however competent individual civil servants might be. In 1846, when the French Ministry of the Interior had 203,900 employees, the Home Office had 29. In the same year all the departments of the central government combined had 21,305 employees, the French having 932,000. Such government as there was—and the ordinary citizen in peacetime had little occasion to notice the government's existence —was a largely amateur business. Virtually all the 5,000 magistrates were unpaid, as were the officers of the 15,500 parishes. Before reform could be effective the machinery of government had to be renovated and adequately staffed, and only a radical change in public attitude towards government, central and local, could make this possible. The work of Bentham, Chadwick and the early inspectors in preaching and practising administrative efficiency and independence was of the first importance in this situation.

The grip of *laissez-faire* tightened at the turn of the eighteenth and nineteenth centuries as the result of a three-sided conflict between the new entrepreneurial ideal of individualism and competition, Tory paternalism and working class co-operation. The victory of *laissez-faire* was clear by 1800 with the abandonment of wage regulation on one side, and the Combination Acts on the other, and within a very few years individualism had gained very wide acceptance even among its previous opponents. Even the radical Whitbread accepted it as axiomatic that 'the price of labour, like any other commodity, should be left to find its own level' (Perkin, 1969, p.168). No doubt this easy and rapid victory depended upon the weaknesses of opposing philosophies. One of the implications of the contemporary agrarian revolution was that ownership of land should be considered as a business rather than a trust and, by accepting this viewpoint, many landowners had sold the pass for paternalism long before the doctrine of *laissez-faire* was enunciated in its complete form. The working class, too, was in a disorganized, intermediate state. The old style urban community based on guild control of domestic industries was obsolete, and the new urban proletariat had not yet realized its existence. A generation had to pass before the embryo of a distinct urban working class culture began to emerge, and longer still before it achieved a coherent political programme and organization.

But, although *laissez-faire* was unchallenged at the level of political action until the 1830s and 1840s, and held its grip at the philosophical level for much longer, we must be careful not to think of it, even at its height, as a wholly coherent programme. In practice it is difficult to find anyone who consistently advocated complete government inaction, if only because in the—by twentieth-century standards— undergoverned state of the country, everyone had first hand experience of the consequences of such consistency. The great majority,

while opposing state intervention *a priori*, were prepared to countenance exceptions in particular cases. Sir Robert Peel, himself a
manufacturer, was responsible for two Factory Acts in 1802 and
1819 and, although it is true that they were largely inoperative, the
fact that Parliament accepted such legislation at this period is in
itself interesting. The abolition of the slave trade commanded all
party support. Even extremists of different parties could support
government action on occasion. Thomas Duncombe, a doctrinaire
Whig, agitated for mining legislation, while Colonel Sibthorp,
among the highest of the Tories, favoured government inspection of
railways. One might expect greater consistency in Bentham, a
political philosopher rather than a politician, but even he found
himself unable to find a wholly coherent position. On the one hand
he could advocate complete individualism, as in his *Introduction to
the Principles of Morals and Legislaion*: 'The community is a
fictitious body, composed of the individual persons who are considered as constituting as it were, its members. The interest of the
community then is, what?—the sum of the interests of the several
members who comprise it.' Or, he could argue against government
action in economic affairs, as in the *Manual of Political Economy*:
'The general rule is that nothing ought to be done or attempted by
government. The motto, or watchword of government on these
occasions ought to be—Be quiet.' On the other hand he could
advocate centralization and efficiency of administration, and neither
he nor his followers were able to resolve the contradiction. Perhaps
most surprising of all, even Edward Baines can be found supporting
state intervention in education (Barnard, 1961, p.104): 'The voluntary principle is inapplicable in education because it is precisely
those who need education most that are least capable of demanding
it, desiring it, or even conceiving it,' Baines, in fact, by his reasoning,
indicates one important reason for his apparent inconsistency. He
was representative of the great mass of contemporary opinion in not
being a doctrinaire supporter of *laissez-faire*, but a man suspicious
of state power for concrete reasons which could be overridden where
a convincing case could be made out, and he was quite astute
enough to put his finger on the critically weak point in the voluntarist
argument on elementary education. It was this characteristic of
early nineteenth-century individualists, that their adherence to
laissez-faire rested on empirical judgments and not on commitment
to dogma, which made it relatively easy for them to shift their ground

when circumstances altered, or when provable hardship was brought to their attention.

Even for the dedicated theoretical supporter of *laissez-faire*, however, a loophole did exist through which the state could exercise some powers of interference, and even control. The point was made by the economist Nassau Senior in his *Suggestions on Popular Education* (1861, p.6):

> I detest paternal despotisms which try to supply their subjects with the self-regarding virtues, to make men by law sober, or frugal, or orthodox. I hold that the main, almost sole, duty of Government is to give protection. Protection to all, to children as well as adults, to those who cannot protect themselves as well as those who can.

Senior and his supporters supposed that the protection to be offered to the great majority of the population would be limited to the protection of the law against crime and violence. It was only later that, under the influence of T. H. Green, a way was found of extending the definition of protection to form a justification for the welfare state. But even on the strictest interpretation, an argument existed for regarding women and children as special cases, along with paupers and lunatics, on the grounds that they could not realistically be regarded as independent economic units.

Nevertheless, even if *laissez-faire* lacked coherence in practice, and even allowed for government action in special cases, there remained in the early nineteenth century a strong presumption against extending the power and influence of government, and in particular against permitting interference by the state in the very wide field reserved for private judgment and responsibility. Education was placed in this category for three separate reasons. First, it clearly fell within the sphere of influence of the parent. Second, the Established Church claimed an historical right of supervision, a claim revived and strengthened against the Committee of Privy Council on Education by the High Church party, represented by Archdeacon Denison. Thirdly, many feared the power of indoctrination offered by state control of education. This fear received its classical statement from John Stuart Mill in his essay *On Liberty*, although by the time he wrote it his view was already being challenged.

A general state education is merely a contrivance for moulding

people to be exactly like one another, and as the mould in
which it casts them is that which pleases the predominant power
in the government . . . it establishes a despotism over the mind,
leading by natural tendency to one over the body.

Nothing like a state education system could possibly emerge in this
country until the presumption in favour of individualism had been
replaced by attitudes more favourable to collective action.

Throughout the nineteenth and twentieth centuries the individualist position has been attacked and undermined from two quite
different directions, although the two attacks have been more or less
contemporary, and have worked towards similar ends. On the one
hand has been the demand for social justice. Experience of the
working of *laissez-faire* soon made it apparent that a policy of
governmental non-interference was not, in reality, so equitable as it
seemed, since it depended upon every competitor in the resulting
contest starting from scratch and it was abundantly clear that they
did not. A wealthy man could afford without undue difficulty to
provide his children, not only with the best available education
involving, very often, contacts with people likely to be useful for
advancement at a later date, but also an environment encouraging
to intellectual development and the acquisition of social competence.
To the poor man the very presence of children might be a crippling
burden, effectively destroying any possibility of improving his own
prospects or standard of living, while the disadvantage of being born
into a poor family could only be overcome by a combination of
exceptional talent, prodigious stamina and sheer good fortune. The
Victorians were quite conscious of the problems raised by use of
restricted linguistic codes, and knew that too many poor children
lacked not only education but educability (*Minutes of the Committee
of Council on Education*, 1845, vol. I, p.268):

No greater error can be made in elementary education than to
suppose that, for the education of the poor man's child, nothing
more is required than is needed for our own children. In reality
the task is infinitely more difficult: our own children, by the
contact of their minds with ours, have acquired that familiarity
with the resources of language, those habits of thought, and those
powers of reason and reflection, and those stores of general
knowledge, in which the children of the poor are always found
to be conspicuously deficient. All that we need for our children

is that technical instruction which cannot thus be indirectly obtained.

It was T. H. Green in the 1880s who put together in a coherent philosophical argument what many others believed but could not quite articulate. He maintained that for much of the population, talk of freedom was meaningless, since the conditions of their life prevented them from developing and using whatever qualities they possessed. In order to produce genuine freedom—the term Green used was 'positive freedom'—the state was entitled to so legislate that everyone did, in fact, have the opportunity to employ his talents, rather than merely drag out an existence inescapably limited by poverty and ignorance, even if this involved substantial interference with the liberties, and even the property, of more fortunate citizens. In a lecture given at Leicester in 1881, Green outlined his case (Bullock and Shock, 1956, p.180f.):

> The mere removal of compulsion, the mere enabling a man to
> do as he likes, is in itself no contribution to true freedom . . . .
> If I have given a true account of that freedom which forms the
> goal of social effort, we shall see that freedom of contract,
> freedom in all the forms of doing what one will with one's own
> is valuable only as a means to an end. That end is what I call
> freedom in the 'positive' sense, in other words the liberation
> of the powers of all men equally for contributions to the
> common good . . . . Our modern legislation then with reference
> to labour, and education, and health . . . is justified on the
> ground that it is the business of the state, not indeed directly
> to promote moral goodness, for that, from the very nature of
> moral goodness it cannot do, but to maintain the conditions
> without which a free exercise of the human faculties is impossible.

Green is interesting because of his unusually clear statement of the argument, and because of his powerful influence both on contemporary statesmen and on later social theorists, notably William Beveridge and R. H. Tawney, but it is important to underline that the ideas he crystallized were being acted upon, often with no very clear rationale, long before he wrote. Sheer humanity, revulsion against the observable effects of unrestrained individualism in terms of human misery, led to a considerable dilution of *laissez-faire* from the 1830s onwards.

The second line of attack upon individualism on the other hand, derived its impetus from fears about national security and prosperity. We shall have to examine this attack later in the chapter, but we should note here that it could arise from alarm about either economic or military rivalry, and very often from a combination of both for, to the nationalist, commerce frequently appears as a branch of war. In either case it led to a demand that the state take active measures to see that the talents of its members were fully exploited, and in making this point its advocates found themselves very close to the reasoning of Green, although with a different emphasis. Both arguments—from social justice and from national strength—led to an assault upon the ideal of a society based upon universal competition, and the suggestion of an alternative ideal of co-operation. Both, too, saw the government occupying an active role as the organizer and inspirer of co-operation.

The movement towards state involvement followed the same course in education as in social welfare in general. In the 1830s and 1840s a campaign built up, demanding a more positive attitude by the government towards social problems, and some important initiatives were taken, not least in public education. Progressively, but against considerable opposition and in an unplanned and piecemeal fashion, government involvement increased, the process accelerating in the 1860s when it may be said that the age of *laissez-faire* was over, Gladstone's government of 1868 often being taken as marking the critical change. From the 1880s, when the theoretical position of *laissez-faire* was finally undermined, another acceleration set in, culminating in the early years of this century with the laying of the foundation of the welfare state. The Balfour Act of 1902 passed, it may be remarked by a Conservative government, by establishing a recognizable state education system, albeit with wide delegation of power from the centre, demonstrated the completeness of the revolution in political thought which had taken place since the first appearance of mass elementary education a century before. Since 1900, two world wars, recurrent economic crises accompanied by a continuous decline in England's relative industrial position and the spread of socialism, have completed the shift from individualism to collectivism.

A combination of factors contributed to produce in the 1830s and 1840s widespread alarm about the state of society. The country was subject to a crisis of social conscience, reflected both in the literature of the period and the torrent of official and unofficial reports upon social problems. People had been aware for a long time that the industrial revolution, along with its manifest benefits, brought problems, particularly for the poor, but the reaction had been either to appeal to enlarged versions of time-honoured remedies, or to call in economic laws to justify short term distress on the grounds that it was the inevitable price of progress, or the result of moral obliquity on the part of the sufferers. By the 1830s both these courses were failing to carry conviction. Far more people had seen, or even lived in, industrial towns, and had first-hand experience of the depths of misery experienced by the poor and of their simmering discontent, which frightened those who were not affected by more humanitarian considerations. The economic difficulties of the 1830s and 1840s were especially deep and long lasting, and the appearance of Asiatic cholera drew attention to the fact that uncontrolled urban growth might bring danger as well as discomfort, and that the danger might not necessarily be confined to the slums. Chartism, Owenism, the rapidly expanding radical press, suggested that the urban proletariat was finding a political identity. And far more, and more reliable, information was readily available. Official reports on mines, factories, agriculture and the sanitary conditions of large towns were immensely influential in stirring public opinion, and local reports by such bodies as the Manchester Statistical Society hardly less so. A special feature of these reports was the use of statistics which became something of a craze in the 1830s—the Statistical Department of the Board of Trade was established in 1832, the Royal Statistical Society in 1833, and the Registrar General's Department in 1838. Some of the reports were not as objective as their language and presentation suggest; they were written by men strongly committed to active social reform, but this in no way diminished their effect, which was reinforced by a succession of works of fiction or exhortation by Dickens, Carlyle, Kingsley, Disraeli and a host of lesser writers. Douglas Jerrold summed up the situation by saying that in 1833 no one was thinking about the poor, and in 1838 no one was thinking about anything alse.

The novel feature of social criticism of the period was the very general note of alarm about the working of *laissez-faire*. A philosophy of universal competition was condemned as being a negation of the very idea of society and, in practice, a cover for irresponsibility and exploitation by those who had the power and duty to rule and to protect weaker members of the community. As Thomas Arnold remarked in a letter to the *Hertford Reformer*, 'We stand by and let this most unequal race take its own course, forgetting that the very name of society implies that it shall not be a mere race, but that its object is to provide for the common good of all.' Carlyle, in his characteristically downright manner, wrote in his essay, 'Chartism':

> That self-cancelling Donothingness and *Laissez-faire* should have got so ingrained into our practice, is the source of all these miseries . . . . What is the meaning of the 'five points' if we would understand them? . . . they are inarticulate prayers: 'Guide me, govern me! I am mad and miserable and cannot guide myself! Surely, of all 'rights of man', this right of the ignorant man to be guided by the wiser, to be gently or forcibly held in the true course by him, is the indisputablest.

Carlyle was representative of the great weight of social comment in advocating three points. The government was to take an active and innovatory role in reform. It was to promote popular education —to quote again from 'Chartism', 'To impart the gift of thinking to those who cannot think, and yet who could in that case think; this, one would imagine, was the first function a government had to set about discharging.' Finally the educated classes were to assume the responsibilities of leadership for which their education fitted them and which, under the sway of *laissez-faire*, they had been evading. One might summarize the programme as a demand to return to a corporate society held together by mutual responsibilities and duties, rather than the competitive society—if society was a permissible term—in which the only relationships were through the cash nexus, which Carlyle regarded with particular aversion. But, although many critics agreed in condemning *laissez-faire*, they did so on different grounds. Some, like Carlyle, revolted against what they conceived to be the inhumanity and irresponsibility of industrial society. A common variation on this attitude was a nostalgia for the middle ages. Dislike of the physical ugliness of industrial towns was a powerful factor here, allied to the very common English preference for the rural life, but medieval life, with its guilds, monasteries and feudal system, could be interpreted—from a safe distance—as an object lesson in co-operation. William Cobbett's *History of the Protestant Reformation* was influential in spreading this doctrine, and the Young England movement gave it publicity. At least equally important was a quite untheoretical realization of the sheer immensity of the social problems arising from rapid social and technological change, and the failure of the voluntary agencies, in spite of their efforts, to make any real impression upon them. To people who thought in this way, increased government power might be unwelcome, but it appeared to be an unfortunate necessity, the alternative being the collapse of society. The economic distress of the 1830s and 1840s with the accompanying working class unrest frightened them, and the continental revolutions of 1830 and 1848 suggested to them what might happen here if no action were taken.

A contributory factor of some importance was the election of a Whig government after forty years of virtually unbroken Tory rule. Although Peel and Huskisson had carried some useful legislation in the 1820s, there remained a backlog of social reform built up in the years of reaction following the French Revolution, and the government of Grey and Melbourne entered office in the mood to act as a new broom and with a powerful body of public opinion behind it in doing so. Precedents, critical to the development of state education, were set up by this government. It spent substantial sums of public money in compensating slave owners when slavery was abolished, and appointed inspectors to enforce the terms of the 1833 Factory Act. And once state intervention in social welfare began it very soon acquired a momentum of its own. The men appointed to administer the new welfare measures—Chadwick, Kay-Shuttleworth, Horner, Tremenheere etc.—were men of first-class ability, independence of mind quite unbelievable in modern civil servants and, as their acceptance of their posts showed, strong belief in the efficacy of state enterprise and the necessity of tackling social problems in a professional manner, with disinterested intelligence and detailed knowledge. Although Chadwick harmed his cause by his abrasive personal relations, he and his colleagues, through their ability and integrity, did much to raise the status and public image of the civil service. At the same time, their investigations not only provided unshakeable evidence to support their advocacy of reform, but frequently uncovered and publicized causes of distress incidental to the original enquiry.

The new impact of government upon private life from the 1830s onwards, is illustrated by the quantity and range of important legislation which reached the statute book. The abolition of slavery and the Factory Act of 1833 have already been mentioned. Other industrial legislation included the Mines Act of 1842, the Factory Act of 1844, the Ten Hours Act, the Merchant Shipping Act, and the Inspection of Mines Act. Public health inspired several measures, covering baths and washhouses, burial grounds, lodging houses, adulteration of food, and improvements to towns, in addition to the major Public Health Act of 1848. An Act of 1824 intended to improve the administration of prisons was made effective in 1835 by the appointment of inspectors, and ten years later provision was made for the inspection and financial assistance of juvenile reformatories. The poor law was given a full scale overhaul in 1834, exciting bitter opposition, and an act of 1844 encouraged poor law authorities to form unions for the purpose of establishing workhouse schools. Perhaps more important even than the extensive legislation was the appearance of a rudimentary administrative machinery, at first inspectors of factories, prisons, schools and mines, then embryo government departments wielding considerable power—the Board of Health, the Committee of Privy Council on Education, later the Education Department, the Science and Art Department, the Poor Law Commissioners, the Charity Commission. Not all of these had an easy passage. The powers of the Board of Health were truncated only six years after its establishment, Kay-Shuttleworth at the Committee of Privy Council had to battle against the hostility of Nonconformists on one side and the revived and aggressive Church of England on the other, while the Poor Law Commissioners, nicknamed the 'bashaws of Somerset House', were the focus for attack from Tories and working class movements, often in alliance. But government departments were permanent additions to the political scene, and their powers steadily increased through precedent and administrative decision (Young, 1953, p.47):

> Of facts, which in Gibbon's phrase, are dominant in the general
> system, by far the most significant in this period is the
> emergence of a new state philosophy of which the overt tokens
> are the Factory Acts, Public Health Acts, and the Education
> Minute of 1846.

It is an indication of the strength of the reaction against *laissez-faire* that government involvement in elementary education should make significant progress in this period, since the obstacles in the way of a state education system were peculiarly strong. Not only was there the deeply-rooted fear of the power of indoctrination given to the government's by its control of popular education, but in addition there was the embittered quarrel between the Non-confomists and Anglicans, inflamed at this very time by the rise of the High Church party, reviving the old claim of the Established Church to control education. At the local level the consequences of this quarrel are disputable; co-operation was not impossible, and rivalry, especially in urban areas, sometimes worked to the benefit of the community by producing two schools or more instead of one. But at the national level it was unarguably pernicious. Legislation, intended to produce a rudimentary national system of elementary education, was repeatedly torpedoed by one side or the other, and it required all Kay-Shuttleworth's formidable political gifts to make progress, largely through administrative decisions rather than through parliamentary activity. This was in the face of a virtually unanimous belief that the extension of elementary education was absolutely necessary, and a growing realization that, by one means or another, voluntary effort would have to be guided and assisted by the state if it were to meet the demands made upon it. Nevertheless, progress was made. Public money was voted for the support of elementary schools, and the scope of this support was progressively extended. A government department appeared, assisted by inspectors, to supervise the government grant which, without the passing of any legislation, increased from year to year, at first slowly and then in the 1850s with a speed which alarmed the government into appointing the Newcastle Commission to investigate the situation. By a minute of 1846 the pupil-teacher system was established and, from some points of view, this has a better claim than the treasury grant of 1833 for being considered the foundation stone of a national education system, for it laid the basis of a state licensed teaching profession employed in state supported schools, and drawing part, at least, of their pay from public funds.

Secondary education did not attract government action at this time except for an Act of 1840, making it easier to amend obsolete trust deeds of grammar schools. But there was one development of considerable influence in the creation of a state system. This was the rise to prominence of an idea which appears to have been enunciated in the first place by Coleridge, but which was taken up with enthusiasm by Carlyle, Disraeli, Kingsley, F. D. Maurice, Thomas and Matthew Arnold, eventually becoming a commonplace

of late Victorian social thinking, the idea that the educated classes—
the 'clerisy' in Coleridge's phrase, Carlyle spoke of a 'spiritual
aristocracy'—had the duty to exercise leadership and that their
education should fit them for this responsibility. That education
should be stratified according to social class was not, of course, new;
quite the reverse. What was original was the suggestion that various
grades of school should each be conceived as preparing pupils with
particular skills and attitudes to contribute to the common good of
society, a suggestion which involved placing public schools, grammar
schools, elementary schools, and different grades of private schools
in a fairly precise relationship to one another, and which thus held
the seed of a national system—although certainly not an egalitarian
system of the type to attract support at the present time. Equally
new, and indicative among other things of the spread of the professional ideal, was the idea that responsibility for leadership went
not so much with high birth or extensive property, or even with
wealth, as with education, a suggestion made quite explicitly by
F. D. Maurice (Williams, 1951, p.122):

> all of us have acquired since that time (1848), a new sense of
> our relation to the working class . . . . It did cause us to fear,
> I own, but it was not fear for our property or position; it was
> the fear that we were not discharging our responsibilities,
> greater than those which rank or property imposes, that our
> education laid upon us.

Matthew Arnold was another to take up this point, arguing that
the aristocracy was incapable of leadership and the working class
not yet ready for power, so that leadership must rest with the middle
class. But the middle class must be transformed and enlightened
before it was fit to assume this responsibility and, as he argued in
A French Eton, 'I cannot see any means so direct and powerful for
developing this great and beneficent power as the public establishment of schools for the middle class.'

Public support of secondary schools did not come until the
beginning of the next century and, when it did so, the concept of
socially stratified education had been given a new interpretation,
but the recovery of secondary education began much earlier, and
some characteristics of the revived schools can be best understood
by reference to the conditions prevailing when the revival began. It
has been remarked (see Simon, 1965, ch. III) that the social stratifi-

cation of education hardened in the mid-nineteenth century. Up to a point this may be explained by the emergence, to which reference has already been made, of the class struggle, although it is inconvenient for this explanation that the movement in schools occurred with particular speed between 1850 and 1870 when, by all accounts, relations between classes were very much less hostile than at any other period in the century. Perhaps more influential was the development which we have just been discussing, by which it came to be taken as desirable that children intended to be the future leaders of society should not only be segregated from their inferiors—this had always been so—but should be gathered together in institutions specifically intended for their education where they could absorb the ethos of the ruling class, and at the same time practice upon each other the skills of leadership which, it was hoped, they would display in later life. The same development offers an explanation, in part at least, of the contemporary shift from private education at home to schooling, and from private schools to public and proprietorial schools. At the census of 1851 private schools still provided for 80 per cent of all children in receipt of secondary education, and as many children were educated at home as at all the public, proprietorial and grammar schools combined. But the best days of the high class private schools were coming to an end as it came to be taken for granted that middle and upper class children would attend the much enlarged and more numerous public schools.

Until the 1860s the developments we have been examining were limited in their impact, interesting to us chiefly as preliminary indications of a coming shift in public opinion, but hardly revolutionary in their own right. Individualism and the Englishman's right to do as he wished with his own, remained pillars of the popular doctrine, and Britain's huge industrial and commercial supremacy allowed most Englishmen simply to ignore the possibility of foreign rivalry. The long period after 1815 without a major European war encouraged an insularity of outlook, reinforced by England's avoidance of revolution in 1848 when disturbance was so general on the continent. The Great Exhibition of 1851 was designed as both a celebration of Britain's industrial power, and the virtues of internationalism and free trade. Only a very few particularly far-sighted people realized that the Exhibition also provided evidence of a growing threat to British predominance, and probably fewer still had any premonition that the age of power politics and nationalism was, within a generation, to bring the beginning of the end for free trade. But by the 1860s the tide was visibly turning. Historians seem to be agreed that Gladstone's government of 1868-74 may be considered as the first modern administration, laying the foundations of the social service state with major reforms to the army, the civil service, the judiciary, public health administration and elementary education. From this period it was no longer possible for a party to seek election with a policy simply of keeping affairs going, and meeting problems as they arose; it had to offer a coherent programme of proposed legislation to have any chance of success. It is not necessary to our purpose to describe, or even to catalogue, the extension of government activity, but the general movement may be illustrated by figures. If allowance is made for changes in price levels, public expenditure on social services in England and Wales increased very nearly six times between 1860 and 1900, or if increase in population be taken into account, the expenditure increased from 4s 7d per head of the population to 16s 7d at constant prices. In the same period the cost of education to public funds multiplied fifteen times. England, committed in the first half of the nineteenth century to a policy, if policy is the word, of non-interference by the government, was moving with accelerating speed towards collectivism.

The underlying cause of this change was an alliance between social justice and national efficiency. We have seen that the mid-century reaction against *laissez-faire* arose from a revolt of social conscience against the suffering of the poor in the process of industrialization, and the apparent indifference of society to these sufferings. Now this revolt was fanned into revolution by political and economic developments. Of these, three are particularly relevant to the study of national education: the relative decline of British industry and commerce; the rise of nationalism and of powerful national states in Europe; and the emergence of the working class as a political power. But we must not think of these as working in isolation; it is only from a distance, and for the purposes of explanation, that they can be separated, and then not with precision. Their interaction was complex, and it is frequently difficult to disentangle cause from effect in discussing them. To take only one example: nationalism arose at least in part because of the appearance of working class political parties, often markedly xenophobic in outlook. But, on the other hand, one of the motives for giving political power to the working class was the hope of contributing to national unity and thus to national strength, while some more Machiavellian politicians were fully conscious that by stirring up nationalist fervour among the working class they might divert them from domestic agitation.

Industrial decline has been discussed previously, in chapter 3, where it was suggested that it produced a demand for expansion of educational provision at all levels to exploit to the full our resources of manpower. All we need to add here is that it was generally assumed that this expansion must be heavily subsidized, if not entirely provided by the government, and that the nationalist and imperialist movements received much support from the belief that industrial recovery required the intervention of the state to back up private enterprise. Indeed the distinction between an economic nationalist and a political nationalist was very fine, and often hardly worth drawing. But, if political nationalism in this country derived some of its momentum from the economic situation, it also had other determinants. The last third of the nineteenth century was a period of rising nationalism all over Europe, not to mention the United States and Japan. The age of power politics may be said to begin with the rise of Prussia in the 1860s, leading to the dictated peace with France in 1871. Bismarck's run of successes against Denmark—involving a severe loss of face by Britain—Austria and France made it clear that in future, victory was going to lie not only with the big battalions but with the big, disciplined, well organized battalions, backed by industrial power. Other European countries took the hint, though none achieved the German success. In Italy, however, the extinction of the Pope's temporal power in 1871 was another example to show that treaties and prescriptive rights were of little consequence when the interests of a great power were concerned, unless backed by adequate force. In the same year, the Russian rejection of the restrictions imposed after the Crimean War on military operations in the Black Sea drove home the same lesson. Britain's acceptance of the Russian action, if anything reinforced the point since it was obvious to all that she lacked the power to do anything else. The British, as a whole, were slow to wake up to the implications of power politics, in spite of the Black Sea affair and the Alabama arbitration of the same year, which again illustrated the limits of British power. It was not until the late 1890s that militant patriotism, rising to hysteria at the time of the Boer War, became a popular movement, but among politicians and intellectuals reaction was quicker in the form of social Darwinism and imperialism.

Social Darwinism was a translation to the sociological sphere of biological theories of natural selection, and drew its ammunition from a rather crude interpretation of the doctrine of the 'survival of the fittest'. It was capable of presentation in contradictory ways. Herbert Spencer's version was that society consisted of competing individuals each of whose survival depended upon being 'fitter' than the rest, thus carrying individualism and *laissez-faire* to their logical limit. The 'external' school, however, believed that competition for survival lay not between individuals but between nations, and (Semmel, 1960, p.31) 'asserted that England's first concern—if she meant to maintain her world position—was with the welfare of her own people, at the expense, if need be, of other inferior peoples.' In this doctrine lay a powerful defence of intense nationalism, and also of imperialism, for it could always be argued that the countries conquered by imperialist nations had been proved, by that fact, to be inferior, and as J. A. Froude observed of England's domination of Ireland (Hayes, 1963, p.12), 'the superior part has the natural right to govern; the inferior part has the right to be governed.' The echoes of Carlyle's teaching in social Darwinism are strong, and indeed the elitist character of social thinking at the end of the nineteenth century, the emphasis upon government by an aristocracy of superior upbringing and education, owes much to the support given by social Darwinism to Carlyle's idea of the 'spiritual aristocracy'. A natural extension of the Darwinian case led to the suggestion that racial improvement might be achieved by selective breeding, but although advocated by Karl Pearson and Francis Galton, eugenics attracted little support except among a few of the Fabians. The more influential interpretation was that for the country to be among the 'fittest' when the test came, it must aim at national unity and the most efficient use of human and material resources. In order to achieve this it must follow a policy of active social reform, not only to avoid the wastage of human potential through unsatisfactory living conditions and lack of education, but also to prevent the destruction of national unity arising from working class discontent.

At this point, the recommendations of the social Darwinists coincided with the calculations of politicians alarmed by the growing threat of socialism. They could see that the Marxist programme was open to attack at two points; it predicted increasing misery for the working class under capitalism, and it advocated an international alliance of the working class against their exploiters. By a policy of state socialism, bringing visible benefits to the workers in the way of pensions, medical services, housing legislation, national insurance, it was hoped to disprove the theory that the poor must always suffer from capitalism, and give them an interest in continued national prosperity. Encouragement of narrow nationalist sentiment served the double purpose of strengthening national unity while, at the same time, undermining the internationalism of the socialist movement, always one of its most vulnerable elements. Bismarck in Germany was the most systematic exponent of state socialism, and it was employed with distinct success in Italy at the beginning of the twentieth century. In this country it was less systematically advocated, perhaps because British working class political movements were not much affected by theoretical socialism. But politicians were fully aware of the advantages to be gained with the working class electorate from pre-empting the reforming position, especially when social reform was allied with imperialism.

For many imperialism was no more than nationalism writ large, and the collection of colonies was a demonstration of national virility, comparable with the collection of gold medals at Olympic games. It was probably this aspect which most caught the public attention; it was gratifying to see so much of the atlas coloured red, and right and proper that Victoria should be Empress of India to balance the Kaiser of Germany and the Tsar of all the Russias. For others it was a philosophy of race, involving the right—even the duty—of certain races to dominate others. But it could be defended on less irrational grounds of hard political calculation. European industries were largely dependent for their raw materials upon imports from underdeveloped countries, and it was an attractive proposition to take political control of these countries, few of which could offer effective opposition, in order to corner supplies of tin, cotton, rubber, oil etc. And once one country started this process, there was a strong pressure upon others to follow suit in self-defence. An added advantage was that colonies offered useful captive markets for the mother country's manufactured goods. To countries like Britain, dependent upon sea communications, certain colonies of little intrinsic value economically were useful for their strategic position or as coaling bases. A special attraction of imperialism to Britain was that it offered a way of compensating for its smallness relative to some of the large nation states which were appearing in Europe and elsewhere. If Britain had a small population compared to Germany or Russia, at least it could call upon the assistance of Canada and Australia, and the huge manpower resources of India. At the time of the Boer War a favourite theme of the popular press was the contribution of units from the Dominions, some compensation for the intense unpopularity incurred on the Continent and in America.

Imperialism and social Darwinism provided powerful incentives for improving health and intellectual development of the population, and it should not be assumed that reform was undertaken simply to keep the working class quiet and forestall the threat of socialism. There was a widespread and quite genuine belief in society's duty to see that all its members lived in conditions permitting them to develop interests and make their maximum contribution to the welfare of the community. But this belief did not imply acceptance of egalitarianism. The favoured model of society was the 'structured democracy', with different social classes playing distinct roles, the direction residing in an aristocracy of talent. In one respect, however, the elitism of Haldane, Morant, and the Fabians differed from that of the middle nineteenth century. It was quite prepared to countenance, even to encourage, promotion from one class to another on merit, in fact it looked to elementary schools to seek out likely candidates for promotion so that potential talent might not be wasted. The Elementary School Code of 1904, issued under Morant's direction, was quite explicit on this point:

> It will be an important, though subsidiary object of the school
> to discover individual children who show promise of exceptional
> capacity, and to develop their special gifts . . . so that they may
> be qualified to pass at the proper age into secondary schools,
> and be able to derive the maximum benefit from the education
> there offered to them.

But those who achieved promotion must be inducted into the ethos of the class to which they had risen, and a major function of the secondary school was to assist in this process. It was a matter of concern to those who thought in this way that the education of children intended for different functions should be clearly differentiated. A secondary education given to a child intended for blue collar occupations would be wasted, since, in Michael Sadler's words, the secondary school 'was chiefly needed by pupils who look forward to a professional career, or to occupying posts of higher responsibility in industrial or commercial life.' If working class children wished to stay at school beyond the minimum leaving age this was to be encouraged, but they should do so in higher elementary schools which, according to Morant, were particularly provided for (Banks, 1955, p.52) 'the continuation beyond the elementary stage, and in a practical direction. of the cleverest children of the working classes.' A succinct summary of the guiding principles of educational policy was given by Sir John Gorst to the British Association in 1901 (Banks, 1955, p.51):

> While primary instruction should be provided for, and even enforced upon all, advanced instruction is for the few. It is the interest of the commonwealth at large that every boy and girl showing capacities above the average should be caught and given the best opportunities of developing these capacities. It is not its interest to scatter broadcast a huge system of higher instruction for any who chose to take advantage of it.

However, if some of the advocates of social reform adopted a position which would today be criticized as undemocratic and elitist, they had no doubts about the necessity of active government involvement. Those of a literary cast of mind found a justification for their belief in the 'organic state' in the writings of Carlyle, developed by Ruskin. Others more influenced by philosophy took T. H. Green and Bosanquet as their mentors. Some of the most influential men of the day—Asquith and Milner are examples—were actually pupils of Green, and his work at Oxford was continued by successive masters of Balliol, Benjamin Jowett and Edward Caird, whose example was acknowledged by Beveridge and Tawney. Many, probably the majority, felt no need for logical justification of their views, taking it as self-evident that for the increase of national power the government must make itself responsible for social reform.

In this belief they were at one with the Labour movement which began to establish a separate political identity in the 1890s, and emerged as a force to be reckoned with in the election of 1906 although, as we have suggested, politicians had been aware for upwards of twenty years of the necessity to appeal to the working class vote. But, naturally enough, the Labour movement approached social reform from a different point of view. The working class was by no means unaffected by militant patriotism; as Austen Chamberlain remarked (Semmel, 1960, p.26) 'the democracy wants two things, imperialism and social reform.' But, while to upper and middle class imperialists social reform was a means to the end of greater national power, to the working man, the sufferer from poor living conditions and restricted life chances, it was an end in itself.

In the context of this study, however, differences of motive are not of the first importance since the consequences for education were the same, a progressive replacement of voluntary by government control, and the establishment of an institutionalized relationship between primary and secondary education—systematization in both of the senses discussed at the beginning of this chapter. The 1870 Act marked a major step in this process, demonstrating the willingness of government at least to 'fill the gaps' in voluntary provision, and setting up local authorities with educational responsibilities. It is an indication of the close relationship between the rise of the modern democratic nation state and the establishment of systems of popular education, that between 1868 and 1881 Britain, Austria/Hungary, France, Germany, Switzerland, Italy, Belgium and Holland all conducted major reorganizations of public education. In the late 1880s some of the urban school boards established embryo education systems, with elementary schools linked by scholarships to higher grade schools, and even to local university colleges. But the critical change came at the turn of the century, when the Board of Education Act and the Balfour Act laid the foundations of a recognizable state system with a central authority exercising substantial powers of initiative and control. These powers were much enlarged in practice by the activity of the Board under Morant. During the 1890s the Education Department had begun to change its attitude from that of a timid and reluctant dispenser of government grant to that of a policy maker and innovator. Its hand was much strengthened in law when it became the Board of Education, and by the elimination of the jumble of authorities claiming some part-time interest in educational administration. An additional indirect source of power lay in the inexperience of the local education authorities which frequently required advice, not to say direction, from the centre, establishing precedents favourable to the future authority of the Board. And, of course, an active and innovating central education authority was in keeping with the political thought of a period which produced the foundations of national insurance, old-age pensions and unemployment benefits, in addition to adding a variety of new functions in the fields of health, welfare and recreation to the education service.

To a man of the 1850s, the England of 1910 would have seemed well on the way to socialism and the government intolerably inquisitorial and disregarding of the traditional liberties of the citizen, but by the standards of the 1970s the impact of government upon the individual was still very slight, and deliberately so. Some progress had been made towards acceptance of the doctrine of the 'national minimum', a level of subsistence below which no member of society should be allowed to fall, and at which public assistance came into operation. But it was assumed that only a minority would be affected, and the idea was by no means dead that recourse to assistance had something shameful about it; it remained in the public mind a charity rather than a right. The current outlook may be illustrated from the educational system. Arrangements existed whereby able students could pass on scholarship from elementary to secondary schools, but most secondary schools had preparatory departments charging fees and drew many of their pupils from this source. When the free place regulations were promulgated in 1907 it was not thought necessary to set up any means test to prevent well-to-do parents from taking advantage of the system, because it was taken for granted that no parent who could avoid it would send his children to an elementary school, a private school or preparatory department being more attractive in spite of the fees because of its prestige and social exclusiveness. In the conditions of the time this assumption was quite justifiable; it was only after the First World War that elementary schools began to attract parents who saw in them a way of securing a free place for their children in secondary school. Before 1914, attendance at a council elementary school did carry a clear working class connotation, and parents seeking an aura of respectability frequently preferred a denominational school in spite of the very distinct advantages enjoyed by council schools in terms of equipment, buildings and staffing.

We cannot embark upon an examination of the causes of the revolutionary increase in the government's powers which has occurred in the last sixty years, but it is relevant to our study to notice that the movement towards collectivism has been much accelerated by the recurrent crises, political and economic, which have been so conspicuous a feature of twentieth-century history. The consequences for social reform of two world wars, and endemic economic troubles involving massive long-term unemployment, have been complex. Numerous examples may be quoted from the field of education alone to demonstrate their adverse effects. Most obvious and long lasting is simple financial inability to afford measures admitted to be desirable. The 1918 Act was made largely futile by the economic crises of the 1920s and early 1930s; raising the school leaving age has been repeatedly postponed; compulsory continuation colleges have never appeared at all; and in the last two or three years, building and development schemes have been cut and staffing ratios affected by financial stringency. Modern war is appallingly expensive. The national debt rose from £650 million in 1914 to £7,435 million in 1920 as a result of the First World War, and a government may be excused if it feels the need for economy after incurring such an outlay, especially when one bears in mind that the ordinary peace time budgets were being balanced at six times the pre-war figure. The effect was probably more intense after the First than the Second World War, because governments of the 1920s were not yet accustomed to calculating in the prodigious sums which have since become almost commonplace. Similarly, in times of widespread unemployment, and between the wars when unemployment figures fluctuated between one million and three and three-quarter millions, it seemed sensible to governments untouched by Keynsian economics to cut back on public expenditure.

War has adverse effects on existing educational facilities as well as upon forward planning. Schools are commandeered, and building and maintenance fall into arrears; teachers are called up and training ceases; evacuation and war work disrupt timetables; blackout and disruption of families, and wartime encouragement of violence and national hatred help to arouse waves of juvenile delinquency; in the Second World War bomb damage to schools was a significant problem. All these factors combine to produce a backlog of improvements necessary to return the situation to its pre-war level, thus exacerbating the financial problems in the post-war years, when a government, already seeking economy, is simultaneously faced by similar demands from other social services. War weariness, too, may produce, as it did in 1918, an overwhelming desire for a 'return to normalcy', which may involve simply returning to the pre-war position, however unsatisfactory, and throwing out along with much specifically war time apparatus, useful experiments capable of application to peace time conditions.

But there is another side. National disasters of twentieth-century dimensions seem to produce in society an attitude of critical self-examination and readiness for radical change. The old order stands condemned for having led the state into crisis, and there is an assumption in favour of reform. At the same time there is a very natural tendency to close ranks. Total war, by definition, affects everybody, and in its light gross social inequalities appear particularly unfair; where sacrifices are equal it seems only reasonable that benefits should be distributed in proportion. H. A. L. Fisher appealed to this sentiment in recommending his Education Bill to the House of Commons in 1918:

> A third feature in the movement of opinion is the increased
> feeling of social solidarity which has been created by the war.
> When you get conscription, when you get a state of affairs
> under which the poor are asked to pour out their blood and to
> be mulcted in the high cost of living for large international
> policies, then every just mind begins to realize that the
> boundaries of citizenship are not determined by wealth, and that
> the same logic which leads us to desire an extension of the
> franchise points also to an extension of education.

Feelings of this kind were very widespread in both world wars, and provided a climate in which proposals for social reform could be sure of a sympathetic hearing. At the same time war helped to break down prejudice against centralization and state enterprise. Where national survival was at stake, as was demonstrably the case in 1916 and 1940 for example, the necessity for centralized direction and restrictions upon individual freedom had to be accepted, and the experience of the last two wars has been that although there may be a reaction against collectivism after the war, as was certainly the case in 1919 and 1920, it never succeeds in returning to the starting point. 'Normalcy' is never quite achieved. To take just one significant statistic, between 1914 and 1923 the civil service increased its staff from 57,706 to 116,241. Thereafter the increase slowed down, but it did not entirely cease; by 1930 there were rather more than 120,000 civil servants.

The increase in central power is clearly visible in both wars. By 1918 the government had instituted conscription and rationing.

Railways and the coal industry had been taken over. Severe financial restrictions had been imposed. One might think, even, of the convoy system as an example of the acceptance of curbs on individual initiative. 1916 was perhaps the critical year with conscription, and the establishment of a ministry of food, and it is Arthur Marwick's opinion that the institution of the War Cabinet in December of that year was the effective beginning of totalitarian government (1970, p. 92):

> In openly accepting the need for greater collectivist control of of the war effort, the War Cabinet moved far beyond the Liberalism which had previously infomed British political practices and into a kind of totalitarianism.

In the Second World War centralization came much earlier and was much more complete; the establishment of a coalition government in 1940 was a indication of the common resolve to sink differences and submit to a powerful central direction. Reaction was also far less marked as the election of a Labour government, committed to a policy of nationalization, in 1945 suggests. Planning for post-war reconstruction began early in the war, and before hostilities had ceased the Beveridge Report had appeared in 1942, the blueprint for the welfare state, supported by White Papers on national insurance and employment, proposals for a national health service and in education, the Norwood Report and the 1944 Act. The legislation establishing the welfare state followed in 1945 and 1946, accompanied by nationalization of several basic industries.

One reason for the ready acceptance of central direction in the Second World War was that the concept of 'planning' had already achieved widespread support in the 1930s. Political and Economic Planning was founded in 1931, and a series of books by members of all parties drove home the necessity for reform to be made a matter of national policy, based upon detailed planning by experts. Arthur Salter's *Recovery* appeared in 1932, Harold Macmillan's *Reconstruction—a Plea for a National Policy* in 1933, Barbara Wootton's *Plan or No Plan* in 1934, and an inter-party group produced *The Next Five Years* in 1935. The economic situation was the fundamental stimulus for this activity. Unemployment running into millions stressed the need for radical solutions, and the problem of the depressed areas underlined the futility of merely local effort. But the popularity of national planning also derived something from contemporary admiration of the Soviet Union and its five year plans, which received publicity from the visits of a number of British public figures, Bernard Shaw, the Webbs, Lady Astor. This was a time when the intellectual Left was beginning to emerge as a conscious political entity—the Left Book Club was founded in 1936—and it exhibited a somewhat uncritical admiration of Russian achievements and methods, the news of Stalin's purges not having yet broken to distress and confuse Communist sympathizers.

In education, the concentration of power at the centre since 1914 has been sufficiently obvious and may be illustrated by a few examples. Perhaps most telling is the change of title from Board of Education to Ministry of Education and again to Department of Education and Science, with corresponding increments in status and prestige for the political head. Also significant is the increasing frequency of government initiative in educational planning. The tripartite system of secondary schooling, the comprehensive re-organization of 1965 and the reaction against this five years later were all imposed from the centre, in the case of the last two against considerable opposition from local authorities and pressure groups of parents and teachers. Colleges of Advanced Technology, plate glass universities and polytechnics are all government creations, or at least their status and siting has been a matter for central decision. One has only to contrast this with the spontaneous local initiative which produced the municipal universities of the 1870s to see what a revolution has occurred in a hundred years. Similarly the extension of teacher training from two years to three, and the institution of the B.Ed. were government initiatives, and at the time of writing a White Paper has just appeared, setting out plans for developments over the next ten years in teacher training, nursery education and several other fields. We need not suppose that all educational ideas originate from Curzon Street, but it has come to be taken for granted that for any particular branch of education there must be a general policy, and that the outlines, at least, of this policy must be laid down by the government.

Earlier in this chapter it was suggested that the decline of *laissez-faire* and its progressive replacement by a popular philosophy of collectivism arose from the pressure of two distinct, but mutually reinforcing, demands for social justice and efficient use of manpower. If we now take an overall view of the developments which we have been discussing we can see that they may be classified under three headings. The first is the systematization of education in both the senses we have employed. By 1902 the skeleton of a national system existed, and since then the articulation has become much closer and control from the centre more powerful. Even where the government is not directly involved, as for example in curriculum design and development, individualism has become unfashionable, particularly since the appearance of teachers' centres and the Schools Council with their heavy emphasis upon team projects and large scale experiments. Examination boards, too, are constantly agitated by the problem of 'comparability'. Even in the independent sector 'independence' is a relative term, since few schools altogether escape the requirements of common entrance and 'O' and 'A' levels. It is really very difficult for a parent to keep his children completely outside the national organization of education except by refusing to send them to school and if he does, he generally faces prosecution since local education authorities are very reluctant to accept anything but formal schooling as education within the meaning of the act.

This brings us to our second heading, the shift of responsibility from parent to community. In theory parents are still responsible for their children's education, but in practice this seems to mean little more than that they may be prosecuted if they do not send their children to school. Any positive action that parents may take is either discounted altogether, or actively hindered by authority. Very few schools have parent-teacher associations enjoying a policy-making, or even a debating function; the tradition is very strong that academic matters are the prerogative of the head and staff. Parents may be informed, but little else. A parent who attempts, shall we say, to change his child's school on any other grounds than geographical removal soon finds how much—or how little — responsibility he really exercises. And if, by chance, he encounters a head sympathetic to his case, he may well discover how little power the school has against the policy makers at 'the office'.

In part this situation arises from nothing more than a defensive attitude of non-co-operation among some teachers, exacerbated by the inflexibility and lack of imagination apparently inseparable from educational administration. Another ingredient, one which frequently stifles parental interest before it starts, is the belief that education, like street lights and dustbin clearance, is one of the services which 'they' ought to provide, a matter for the professionals. If we look at the historical reality, we see that the doctrine of parental responsibility has always been interesting in theory, but largely ignored in practice. The Victorians were driven to compulsory education, against some of their strongest political principles and prejudices, because of overwhelming evidence that poor parents were not undertaking their responsibilities. At the other end of the social scale, headmasters of Victorian public schools were at least as unforthcoming as modern schools in their relations with parents, and far blunter in their expressions of disinterest. In the twentieth century the welfare state has increasingly assumed the protective functions previously, in theory at least associated with the family, so that the habit has grown of looking upon education as yet another welfare service to be provided by the authorities, local or national.

But the elimination of the family from education is not merely accidental. One aspect of the demand for social justice is that one's chances in life should not be determined by the accident of birth into a family or neighbourhood, and the school has been reckoned as one agency for counterbalancing the disadvantages suffered by children from deprived or apathetic backgrounds. An inevitable concomitant of this attitude is suspicion of parental interference in, education. After all, so the argument goes, the home is not an ally but an obstacle in the educational process.

In this respect English schools differ very distinctly, in theory at least, from their American counterparts. The American interpretation of a democratic education system is one which is closely controlled by, and reflects the values of, the community in which it is placed. The English, rather, incline to see the school in a democracy as moderating the effect upon children of birth and locality. Thus the comment that a school is not integrated with the community, while a serious criticism to an American teacher, might be taken in England to be praise if it implied that the children were thereby freed from the limitations of their upbringing. It is not for us here to attempt to arbitrate in this question, but merely to note the significance of the English attitude in encouraging schools to be independent of parental opinion.

Finally, the scope of the education service widens. It is not so much that the academic content of the school curriculum expands, although of course this does occur, but rather that activities not previously thought to come within the school's orbit at all are added to its responsibilities—organized games and physical education, school meals, medical examination and treatment, careers advice, probation reports, youth clubs, outdoor activities, sex education, protection against the mass media, counselling—the list lengthens all the time. Very often the school becomes the venue for such activities more or less by accident. It happens to be the one place at which all children must sooner or later appear, so that is a convenient centre for medical examinations, meetings with vocational guidance units etc. In other cases the advantages of using schools are admittedly disputable. Some youth leaders maintain, for example, that youth clubs are more likely to attract young people if they are not attached to schools with their associations of pupil status and imposed discipline. But, on the other hand, schools possess amenities very useful to youth clubs—stages, gymnasia, canteens and so on, and duplication is very expensive. So we must beware of supposing that the extension of school activities is always the result of some deliberate policy of social engineering; it may simply be a balance of administrative convenience. Nevertheless, whether or not such activities are offered in school, they are almost invariably offered by public authorities and demonstrate, once more, how the details of private life have been brought within the area of national planning. It is this development which makes it so hard for anyone to avoid formal institutional education, or even, for most people, to conceive the possibility of doing without it.

Chapter 6

The implications for de-schooling

Before attempting to assess the implications of an historical perspective for the de-schooling case, it may be useful to draw together some of the principal points which have been suggested in the last three chapters. And the first point which emerges, with great clarity, is that educational expansion is caused by a multiplicity of factors interacting in very complex ways. It is inviting in such a situation to take a reductionist line, attributing all educational development to say, the demands of industry and commerce, or to an attempt to strengthen social or political control. But, however superficially inviting, this must be resisted, for simplicity can only be obtained at the cost of distortion. Although voices, often influential voices, have repeatedly called for expansion and tighter organization of education to meet the needs of the economy, the practical results of these demands have, until the past twenty years, been surprisingly meagre, and it is interesting to see that the White Paper, *Education: A Framework for Expansion*, published in December 1972, speaks of a shift in emphasis in higher education away from science and technology towards arts and the human sciences, while stressing the liberalizing aspect of higher education as against vocational preparation. So, even today, one must beware of attaching too great an importance to economic causation.

On the other hand, and this illustrates the difficulty of achieving simple, all embracing explanations, while the direct demand of the economy for trained personnel has not until recently been excessive, some indirect consequences of economic expansion have been important. One of these was a massive expansion of what may be called pre-professional education, the production of young people able to profit from on-the-job training at all levels of careers from semi-skilled to professional. In addition, and it is a fundamental point, only the revolutionary economic expansion of the nineteenth and twentieth centuries made it possible to extend formal education to the whole population.

It is not merely that the causes of educational change are numerous; from time to time the emphasis shifts, sometimes rapidly and completely, so that it may be very misleading to argue from the conditions of one period in order to explain developments in another. A very clear example is the use of schooling to establish social or political stability. In the early nineteenth century this was perhaps the most frequently expressed motive for founding elementary schools, whose function was conceived as the production of sober disciplined and industrious workers well disposed towards the political and religious establishment. For this period, although one may easily exaggerate the degree of consensus prevailing among advocates of elementary schooling, a conspiracy theory of motivation, attributing the provision of schooling to a conscious attempt by the establishment to keep the working class in its place, has something to recommend it. Certainly such motives were explicitly avowed by numerous influential writers and politicians. From the 1850s onwards a progressive liberalizing of outlook occurred, but well into the twentieth century the very obvious division of function between schools whose alumni were intended for leadership and those which aimed to produce followers, suggested that older ideas still retained much of their force. Unfortunately it is not clear what this tells us about schools at the present time. It is historically interesting that political indoctrination should figure so prominently among motives for school provision in the early nineteenth century, but we are urged to de-school *now*, and we need to base our decision upon the contemporary functions of schooling, not those of a hundred or more years ago.

If we are in doubt about the extent to which the function of education in society shifts with time, an instructive example is provided by the relation of education to social class. Until the late nineteenth century the system determining social status was conceived of as 'aristocratic'. That is to say, the chief determining factor was birth, and education served to prepare a child for his previously established place in society. By the end of the century the concept of 'meritocracy' was well developed. This accepted the existence of social stratification, but gave to education the task of deciding which children were to be allocated to different classes, academic achievement being the first criterion. From the 1890s onwards continuous efforts were made to refine the selection process, widen the pool from which candidates were drawn, and eliminate bias due to accidents of birth. Within the last fifteen years halting and irresolute approaches have been made towards an egalitarian organization of education, in which the schools' function is not to conform or select for social class, but to eliminate it. We must not suppose that any system—aristocratic, meritocratic or egalitarian—has ever existed in its ideal form. The concept of meritocracy, for example, has never been entirely absent from English educational thinking. Nevertheless, quite distinct differences in emphasis are observable between the 1850s, the 1900s and the 1960s in orthodox attitudes towards the relationship between schooling and social status.

Another matter which impresses itself upon us is the necessity of looking behind declared motives for educational development to see what was really happening in the schools. The implication here is not that the founders of schools were engaged in deliberately deceiving society about their intentions, for very often they were as much deceived as anyone else. Confusion arises at several levels. First there is the now familiar distinction between the 'manifest' and the 'hidden' curriculum of a school. It is a sufficiently well-known pedagogical phenomenon that the inculcation of values and attitudes in pupils is frequently most efficiently done indirectly. Direct moral teaching tends to build up consumer resistance which may be avoided where the code of values is picked up unconsciously in passing. The tone and organization of a school are very effective indoctrinators, the more so since their influence is largely subliminal, and children's personalities may be very much affected by such factors as the quality of relationship between staff and pupils—*laissez-faire*, authoritarian, paternal, hostile, egalitarian etc.—or between senior and junior pupils. Whether a school stresses competition and individual achievement, or co-operation and mutual support, whether or not it encourages pupils to think of themselves as an *élite* or as predetermined followers, may have important consequences upon their development.

The manifest and hidden curricula may work in the same direction, indeed they may even be deliberately designed to do so for, although it is only recently that the 'hidden curriculum' has been written of under this name, its existence has long been known to teachers, and employed as an educational agent. The routine and organization of a monitorial school, for example, was peculiarly suited to assist in the production of a disciplined, industrious work force, a fact well understood by contemporary commentators. Similarly, the late nineteenth-century public schools and early twentieth-century grammar schools made conscious use of the school ethos to reinforce their elitist character. But it is very possible for the school's ethos to work against its expressed intentions, and this, obviously, is very likely to occur where little or no attention has been paid to the effects of school organization or teacher expectation upon pupils' attitudes. One thinks immediately of comprehensive schools where social mixing, regarded as so important by advocates of comprehensive education, is effectively prevented by rigid streaming, or the many schools which preach the virtues of co-operation, but lay great stress in practice upon individual achievement, reinforced by class lists, prizes, competition for success in sport etc.

A second source of confusion is the apparently inescapable liberalizing effect of education. While it is easy to find numerous examples of writers and teachers who believed that schooling could be used as a means of social control by inculcating subordination and contentment with one's social position, it is very hard to see that schools ever, in practice, succeeded in performing this role. That they exercised a civilizing influence is clear, making their pupils literate and articulate, expanding their power of concentration and their ability to co-operate, and introducing them to the possibility of sustained intellectual work. But, while they often used rigid disciplinary techniques and teaching methods based heavily upon rote learning, and while they frequently saw their role as that of defenders of the status quo, one of the principal results of their efforts was to raise their pupils' levels of aspiration, while they conspicuously failed to prevent them from questioning the social and political establishment. On the whole, the evidence strongly favours those who contended that the effect of mass schooling upon society was that of an irritant rather than a soporific.

But this brings us to the point, very important in this study, that the power of schooling to form personality is not so great as it has often been supposed to be both by advocates and critics of institutional education. Even today, when compulsory school attendance extends for eleven years, children are exposed to a wide range of alternative and potentially competing influences, family, various peer groups, the youth culture, mass media etc. The resultant of all these different pressures is almost impossible to predict, and the influence of the school must inevitably be diluted; it is not at all certain that the school is even the predominant, let alone the sole, factor. At any previous period the proportion of the population attending school was smaller, and the length of stay shorter, producing a corresponding reduction in the school's influence.

Thus it is very unsafe to argue in education from stated intentions to actual results. Knowledge of the educational objectives of teachers, school managers, politicians etc., is of value in itself, particularly as a guide to contemporary notions about the ideal relations between schools and society. Shifts in such objectives, such as the one recently mentioned, from an aristocratic to a meritocratic ideal, and then to an egalitarian one, are useful indices to major changes in social theory which will have a powerful effect upon schools, although one very hard to predict, or even to assess afterwards. But it is an open question how much we learn from these about what the schools actually did. Indeed so many contributory influences bear upon the development of children that it is difficult, perhaps impossible with any precision, to distinguish the effects of education. When we look at a comparatively specific social change such as the spread of temperance in the late nineteenth century, we find Sunday schools and elementary schools conducting regular campaigns to reduce drinking, reinforced by massive propaganda efforts directed at adults. Alongside these must be considered the effects of licensing laws and, less direct but possibly even more powerful, factors such as improvements in housing, provision of alternative methods of recreation, better working conditions and the spread of elementary education. Precisely what part elementary schools played in attacking the massive drink problem of the nineteenth century is a matter of little more than speculation, and it is hardly easier to say whether specific temperance propaganda was more effective, even within schools, than the more general civilizing effect of compulsory education. With this example in mind it is as well to exercise care in attributing large social changes, benign or otherwise, to education and the less specific the change in question the greater is the need for caution. Of course, it follows that if we can only with much doubt describe what the social functions of education have been in in the past, at least equal diffidence must be felt about anticipating the future consequences of schooling.

But it is possible to make a fundamental mistake in attempting to interpret the effects of education, which makes the task quite unnecessarily difficult. This is to over-emphasize the strictly conservative element in the ideology of teachers and educationalists. When one scrutinizes the motives expressed by such people, one finds that they invariably involve some social change which seems necessary to the sponsors. The proposed change may be reactionary, in the sense that it is a return to some suitably idealized version of the past, or it may be based upon a similarly idealized view of a technological or egalitarian future. Mere retention of the existing situation, however, rarely if ever figures as a motive for founding schools. Hannah More and her contemporaries, for instance, were not saying that the working class *do* respect their social superiors and that their children should be taught to follow in their footsteps. Their whole point was that the working class *ought* to show respect and obedience but did not, and that it was necessary to aim an educational crusade at their children in order to return to the right ways of a generation or so ago. Similarly, present-day advocates of comprehensive schools do not recommend them on the grounds that society is egalitarian and that schools should reflect this, but rather that society is not egalitarian but should be so, and that schooling may be an agent in bringing about this end. The fact is that it is far more illuminating to think of education as a counterbalance to received opinions and values than as a reinforcement for them, provided that one bears in mind the warning about the dubious connection between intentions and results. When one adopts this viewpoint it becomes easier to understand why, as was noted above, education so often acts as a social irritant.

One other matter should be emphasized in this summary—the close relation between the spread of formal schooling and a move towards a collectivist and egalitarian community. The critical period for the institutionalization of education came at the turn of the nineteenth and twentieth centuries, with the establishment of compulsory schooling and a recognizable national system of education, however 'system' is interpreted, and this corresponded with the visible and quite deliberate replacement of the *laissez-faire* community based upon individualism and a negative attitude towards government, by a new style of collective, centralized state. Since then the power of the central government, and its willingness to initiate social policy has progressively increased, and so has the institutionalization of education and its involvement in national planning. Up to a point the relationship is quite obvious, although certainly not trivial, since only a modern industrial state with a highly centralized administration can afford an educational system of the extent to which we are now accustomed. But there is more to it than this, for, although a modern industrial state can afford such an educational system, it is not logically necessary that it should do so; its members must feel that the investment is worth making.

In this context public education is seen as serving two general functions; it acts as a 'capacity-catching machine', to use Sidney Webb's phrase, and it serves to counteract inequalities arising from family background. The first of these functions, although historically important, is not of particular consequence to the controversy over de-schooling, but the second is central to the argument and must be discussed later in this chapter. Here it is enough to point out that from its beginning, public education has been advocated as a means of escape for children from the limitations of their native environment. Until recently the emphasis has been upon its capacity to assist the talented and determined individual to become socially mobile, but this is being replaced, to a degree at least, by the notion that social disadvantage may be more generally removed, or at any rate mitigated, by education, the school thus being seen as an agent of egalitarianism. This is clearly in direct contradiction to the de-schoolers' criticism that public education serves to fit people for pre-determined positions in technological society.

If we now attempt to summarize the results of a historical perspective upon the de-schoolers' case we find that some, at least, of their assertions are confirmed. The initial phenomena to which they draw attention certainly exist. Childhood and youth have emerged as stages of life, each with an independent consciousness and institutions, and schools have taken over as the typical educational agency to the point at which the words 'schooling' and 'education' have become virtually synonymous except in specialist discussion. Further, the evidence does suggest that distinctive institutional treatment of childhood and youth has been an important factor in producing this autonomy. Most significantly, one can detect a quite uncritical acceptance of the desirability, indeed the necessity, of organizing and institutionalizing not only education but also other activities of young people, and bringing them within the scope of national planning. Economists are perhaps less committed than ten years ago to the value of indiscriminate extension of education as a national investment; recently they have expressed alarm about the apparently irreversible rise in the proportion of national income allotted to education. But there is no sign of any weakening of the common conviction that the answer to social problems of youth is to offer a yet wider range of organized and structured leisure time activities. Indeed 'education for leisure' is one of the currently fashionable phrases, and we may expect expansion in this field. Another movement which is clearly gathering strength is for closer relations between school and community, by involving parents and other adults in school functions, and conversely by engaging pupils in community affairs, often outside normal school hours. The effect, again, is to widen the sphere of influence of the school. But the most obvious case of expansion is the raising of the minimum school leaving age, which is to be compounded in the near future by a new provision of nursery schools.

One criticism of the modern educational scene offered by the de-schoolers is that teaching has become a professional monopoly, and once more our study confirms that this is a fact, leaving its implications on one side for the present. And further, it is a new development, significantly accelerating in very recent years. Until the appearance of the pupil-teacher system in 1846 training for teaching hardly existed, and one could not usefully speak of a teaching profession. At all levels people took up and dropped teaching without any formality, and generally without apparent consciousness of the need for any preparation. Running a private elementary school was a notorious last resort for men who, through incompetence or physical disability were unable to follow any other trade, and it was common practice to run such a school as a sideline to other businesses. At the secondary level, possession of a degree was generally thought necessary, or at least desirable, but nothing more. Young clergymen regularly took employment as tutors while waiting for a benefice and, later in their career, a headmastership was a recognized stepping stone to a bishopric. During the nineteenth century, training through the pupil-teacher system, and often through college, was slowly established as the normal way to become an elementary school teacher, although untrained teachers remained numerous until after the Second World

War, but training for secondary school teachers did not begin until this century and was for long regarded with suspicion by many headmasters. Now, however, we have regulations requiring training for teachers in state schools, and the period of training has been progressively increased. The private sector remains, of course, and employs many untrained teachers, but even this is subject to government regulations and is at present threatened with take-over in the interests of equality of educational opportunity. Independent schools are certainly vulnerable to attack on the grounds that they perpetuate the privileges deriving from wealth, but the fact remains that their elimination would virtually complete the educational monopoly of the professionally trained teacher.

A centralizing trend is also very clear. Control of even low grade decision making is being removed from the teacher and school to central agencies, and the power of the government over major decisions has increased, in part at least, due to its control over the financial resources necessary to meet the ever rising cost of education. The main significance of the progress from Education Department, through Board of Education and Ministry of Education to Department of Education and Science has been the increasing willingness of central government to dictate educational policy to local authorities in line with more general political programmes. The imposition of comprehensive reorganization, and its subsequent discouragement are clear cases of purely political decisions by the central government, made effective where necessary by pressure upon local authorities. Another is the destruction of the Burnham Committee's precarious claim to independence by repeated governmental dictation of settlements. All in all, education has been brought very firmly within the orbit of national policy.

Individual teachers find their autonomy reduced both by tighter administrative control as, for example, by the much enlarged advisory staffs of local authorities, and by the introduction of large scale co-operative schemes for the reform of curriculum and method. Tighter administrative control reverses the previous trend, which since the days of 'Payment by Results' has been towards greater independence for the teacher, a development made possible by the appearance of the trained assistant teacher, an innovation of the 1870s. The reversal arises partly from increased size of schools. Where one teacher taught all the history in the school, or all the children in one year, he could extemporize or experiment as he wished without throwing the whole school out of gear. Now, when a dozen or more teachers may be involved in one area of teaching, close organization is necessary if different groups of children are to be kept anywhere near in step or follow a connected syllabus. The same is true where co-operative methods of teaching are used, whether one is thinking of team teaching involving only two or three members of a staff, or of a massive curriculum development exercise engaging many schools.

So far we have only considered uniformity of approach as a by-product of increasing scale of organization. But behind the fashion for team teaching, integrated studies, co-operative development projects, etc., one can detect a conscious policy based upon an assumption that for teachers to work in committee is good in itself and that isolation, whether of teacher or subject, is somehow disreputable and undemocratic. We notice, as another example, how many text books today are produced by consortia of scholars and teachers; the Open University is a trend-setter in this direction. It may be, of course, that several heads are really better than one, and that all the unkind remarks that have been made about committees do not apply in education. No doubt these particular committees are strictly democratic, and the will of the majority prevails and is recorded in their curricula and reports. But still, such group projects inevitably restrict opportunities for individual innovation; the lone wolf may be muzzled in committee. And the uneasy thoughts remain that the virtues of co-operation are accepted uncritically and without examination, and, perhaps more important, as political and religious leaders have always known, group sessions are a prime method of suppressing heterodox opinions. When we add the enlarged advisory staffs referred to above, and recommendations for compulsory in-service training, we have the machinery for the imposition of pedagogical uniformity. Whether this machinery is used at present or not is irrelevant; critics are entitled to point out that it exists, and that very few teachers, or indeed anyone else, seem to be aware of its possibilities.

We must allow, therefore, that the de-schoolers have made out a prima facie case. They have drawn attention to certain features of the educational picture which deserve a more critical appraisal than they have so far received. But when we do conduct such an appraisal, we do not necessarily arrive at their conclusions. One of the advantages of an historical perspective is that it allows us to see why an educational institution has taken one particular form rather than another. We can examine the situation existing before the institution appeared, discover the hopes of its founders and compare them with its achievements, trace its reforms and perversions, and perhaps most important from a practical point of view, make an informed guess at what might happen if it were removed. This is of some consequence in an enquiry like the present one because in criticizing any institution it is necessary to be clear what is its rationale. Sociologists point out that an institution may be dysfunctional from one point of view, or for one group, yet functional for others, and this should remind us that it is possible to make perfectly valid criticisms of such an institution which do not amount to a case for abolition because they ignore the real reason for its existence.

The general function of schooling, so the de-schoolers assert, is to prepare children for technological society first by equipping them with the technical skills demanded by industry, and second and more important, by so indoctrinating them that they are incapable of questioning the values upon which such a society rests (Reimer, 1971, p.19):

> School has become the universal church of a technological society, incorporating and transmitting its ideology, shaping men's minds to accept this ideology, and conferring social status in proportion to its acceptance. There is no question of man's rejecting technology. The question is only one of adaptation, direction and control.

In more detail (Reimer, 1971, p.23):

> schools of all nations, of all kinds, at all levels, combine four distinct social functions: custodial care, social role selection, indoctrination, and education as usually defined in terms of the development of skills and knowledge.

Let us take these four categories as a basis for discussion in the light of our historical survey.

We are not likely to dispute the truth of the statement that schools exercise custodial care of children. This has always been one of the cardinal functions of schools, especially of schools for young children; in fact it was virtually the only function of the cheap private schools of the eighteenth and nineteenth centuries, which drew the bulk of their trade from working women who wished to have those children who were too young to work taken off their hands. But, although we may be prepared to accept the fact of schools' commitment to custodial care, the implications of it are not so clear. Reimer's comments (1971, pp.23-35) revolve about the high proportion of the educational budget allotted to custodial care rather than to 'instructional activities', and upon the effect of such treatment in establishing an autonomous stage of 'childhood' and extending it to the whole population. So far as the cost is concerned it is necessary to drew attention to an undeclared assumption which underlies the de-schoolers' arguments in this and other contexts, namely that the only legitimate function of a school is passing on technical skill and knowledge, other purposes being at best time wasting, at worst sinister. When Reimer refers to authorities who assert that 'in Puerto Rico less than 20% of a teacher's time is available for instructional activities. The rest is spent on behaviour control and administrative routine' or that in the USA 'everything a high school graduate is taught in twelve years of schooling could easily be learned in two years and with a little effort in one', it is obvious that the definitions of 'instructional activities' and 'learning' have been deliberately narrowed for polemical purposes to exclude all the process of socialization that many schools consider their prime purpose. An infant teacher, for example, would probably wish to claim that much of her effort was directed to helping children make the transfer from the enclosed and protective environment of the family to the larger and more complex society outside, and this does not seem to fit very happily into either of Reimer's categories. Neither, for that matter, do music, art, literature or physical education. In fact, a division of a teacher's time into the two categories of 'instructional activities' and 'behaviour control and administrative routine' does not correspond with the reality of the situation at all, unless one is prepared to allow a very wide definition to one class or the other, thus demolishing the grounds of the original complaint about cost. We notice that Reimer himself wishes to include 'indoctrination' and 'social role selection' among a school's functions, and while indoctrination might be classed under 'instructional activities', social role selection presents the same problems of classification within his framework as music or physical education.

But even if, to advance the argument, we allow a very wide connotation to 'custodial care' to cover the passing on of social competence, and if we further agree that schools do spend much time, effort and money in this area of work, perhaps even to the detriment of academic or technical achievement, we still face the question whether they are wrong to do so. Really there are two questions here. Should this work be attempted at all? And, if so, who should do it? Reimer is of the opinion that much custodial care could be dispensed with:

> Children must, of course, be cared for—if they really are children, that is, and not just young members of the community taking part in its normal productive and social affairs. Most youngsters still get along without special care, all over the world, in the tribal, peasant and urban dwellings of the poor.

But this immediately encounters several strong objections. Common sense revolts on at least two counts. It is true that most youngsters get along without special care. Most youngsters, unfortunately, get along on an inadequate diet. They have to. But while this is an admirable argument for improving the dietary of the unfortunate, it is no argument at all for starving everybody. The evidence of sociology confirms what common observation would suggest, that the effect of an upbringing without special care among the urban dwellings of the poor is more likely than not to stunt children, physically, intellectually, aesthetically and morally. And one may question, too, whether women should have their social and industrial roles unavoidably restricted by responsibility over a long period of years for children. It is significant that much of the present pressure for increased nursery school provision comes from women who wish to have the opportunity of a career or fuller social life rather than be tied to child minding.

A more strictly historical objection is closely related. An upbringing limited to the kind of informal socialization of which we are thinking, may be adequate to a society in which change is negligible and the range of situations encountered by an adult is restricted and predictable. Where upbringing is more open-ended and the society into which children are to be inducted is complex and rapidly changing, the socialization process must be longer and more deliberately structured to produce flexibility of response. A comparison between rural and urban life illustrates the position. Even today it is possible for people of very limited intelligence to live a more or less normal life in a small village where the social requirements are routine, and everyone knows them and is aware of their restricted capacity. In a town such people almost inevitably have to be placed in an institution for their own protection because of the complexity of the situations they have to face.

When Reimer writes that (1971, p.24) 'The really important consequence of packaging custody with the other functions of the school is the extension of childhood from age twelve to twenty five, and from the sons and daughters of the rich to the youth of the whole society', our response is once more ambivalent. It does seem to be historically true that the separate institutional treatment of children and young people has been instrumental in crystallizing a conscious culture of childhood and youth, but it does not necessarily follow that this development is entirely bad. That it poses problems, especially for higher education, is certain, for colleges and universities now find themselves dealing with students who are biologically and legally adult, and it is equally certain that these problems have not yet been resolved. It is also true that the wider social and intellectual distribution of secondary and higher education raises problems which have not always been honestly faced by educational policy makers. But if we allow all this, does it amount to a case for de-schooling? Is it self-evidently right that young people should be forced into adult occupations and adult responsibilities at the earliest possible moment? One of the fundamental tenets of Rousseau, repeatedly reinforced since his time by other 'progressive' educators is that children should be encouraged to work out their childhood before being obliged to become adult. And no one could accuse the progressive educators of whole-hearted approval of modern technological society. In Rousseau's time, of course, the economic situation was such that an extended childhood was out of the question for most children; they had to be out earning a living as soon as they were physically capable. The industrialization of society has made it possible for the privilege to be extended far more widely, and the question must be asked, if it was right for the 'sons and daughters of the rich', on what grounds is it wrong for 'the youth of the whole society'?

The de-schooling case here rests upon the assertion that keeping young people in full-time education is a way of depriving them of their political, legal and economic rights (Reimer, 1971, p.24):

So long as children remain full-time students they remain

children—economically, politically, even legally . . . . The
school schedule remains, also, one of the major supports for
age restrictions on the right to vote, to work, to contract, and to
enjoy other constitutional privileges and protections.

Now, whatever the situation may be in the United States or elsewhere, this is simply untrue so far as this country is concerned.
Indeed, within the last few years, just as the great explosion of higher
education has begun, the age of majority has been lowered from
twenty-one to eighteen, thus enfranchising at a stroke virtually all
students at university and college. What is more, one of the reasons
for taking this step was that politicians became aware of the eighteen
to twenty-one age group as a distinct section of society with its own
views and interests, a consequence as we have seen of institutional
education.

A further historical observation suggests itself. It is certainly the
case that care of children has been institutionalized, and that control
of schools has been centralized; but an important reason for this is
bitter experience of the alternatives. Free enterprize in child minding
was tried in the eighteenth and nineteenth centuries, as it was in the
care of the physically and mentally sick and the poor, and the result
was not encouraging. The laws of free competition worked predict-
ably; those who could afford to pay well received good value; the
plight of the others is recorded by Dickens and the Commissions of
Enquiry of the 1830s and 1840s. One of the most important lessons
learned by the Victorians was the necessity, if corruption and
inefficiency were to be avoided, of close supervision backed by the
formation of codes of professional conduct. Modern schools,
hospitals, and asylums are not beyond criticism, and scandals do
occur, but it is simply perverse not to recognize the prodigious
improvements which have occurred since the private asylums and
baby farming of the early nineteenth century. The twentieth century
has many unamiable characteristics, but it is only just to record that
the welfare state, for all its imperfections represents an acknowledge-
ment of public responsibility for those in need of assistance which
was not achieved two centuries ago. It also, and the point is
relevant to our discussion, represents a financial outlay only possible
in a developed industrial state.

Like custodial care, social role selection is well established as
one of the basic duties of modern schools. In this country the
school's influence is still surprisingly limited. Not only can accidents

of birth override the effects of schooling, but birth into one family or another still determines to a great degree what type of school a child will attend, and how successful he will be there.

Nevertheless, it is obvious that children's careers, and thus their social standing, are decided very largely by their education, and especially by their success or otherwise in being selected for a grammar school type of course at eleven, and for higher education at eighteen. Much has been written about the inefficiency of the selection process with its consequent wastage of talent, and the de-schoolers are not alone in drawing attention to the cost of the system in terms of children's experience of failure, its self-confirming character, and its tendency to imbue even the successful competitors with a worship of success rather than of excellence. All this is true and important. An historical view cannot qualify these criticisms, but it does suggest some explanation, if not a justification, of the present state of affairs.

Social selection has not always been an important task of schooling. Until well into the nineteenth century the social role of education was rather to confirm a selection process already conducted through the chance of birth. Schools drew their pupils from very homogeneous backgrounds, and taught them a social code suited to their rank. Some marginal mobility did occur. Parents might purchase for their children an education rather above their real station in the hope of assisting them to rise; public and proprietarial schools served this function for middle class children whose parents wished to put them into contact with the gentry and upper professions. In a few extreme cases—perhaps less often in the nineteenth century than formerly—a child of poor parents might be sponsored at a school well beyond his family's financial or social reach and so achieve promotion, but here it was the sponsor rather than the school which produced the mobility. It was only in the mid-nineteenth century that, in a deliberate attempt to widen the field of available talent and break the stranglehold of nepotism upon public appointments and promotion, educational qualifications came to be used as criteria of selection. By the end of the century the concept of schooling as a 'capacity-catching machine' had become an orthodoxy, and although criticisms were often made of its working, the principle was hardly challenged until the last few years, critics being chiefly interested in ensuring that the method of selection was not biased against working class children.

The criticism which is now made is that, while selection upon educational achievement may be preferable to nepotism in that it does allow for social mobility, the whole concept of social mobility pre-supposes that social stratification is a more or less permanent characteristic of society. Might we not, so the argument goes, substitute for the selfish notion of individual social betterment— implying a corresponding failure on the part of the majority—a concern for the betterment of the whole working class? And for this is it not necessary to imbue children not with the competitive values of social mobility, but with the co-operative values of class consciousness? One does not have to accept the full Marxian working-out of the case to see that there is some force in the contention that the school system, as at present organized and administered, has built into it an inescapable ethos of individual competition, and that while selection and promotion are on an individual basis the competitiveness is hardly ameliorated by including team games and group projects in the curriculum. The purely practical problem, however, is that while demand for secondary and higher education exceeds the supply, it is hard to see how some form of selection is to be avoided, and nineteenth-century experience suggests that the alternative to educational selection is likely to be not the open society, but the return of nepotism.

'Indocrination' is an emotive word with strong pejorative connotations, and it can be used so loosely as to lose most of its meaning and become merely a term of abuse. But the de-schoolers are, in fact, quite precise in their usage. When they speak of the school as an agent of indoctrination, they mean that it has been used to so condition or brainwash its pupils that as adults they are unable to question the fundamental assumptions of modern technological society, or to conceive of radical changes to it. This is an assertion which lends itself particularly to validation or otherwise by an historical examination. It is relatively easy to frame questions which may be tested against the expressed motives of educationalists, and politicians, and against the observable consequences of mass education over a period of more than a century. When we do this we find results which are illuminating partly because they contain contradictions. We do not find that education has been advocated specifically on the grounds that it indoctrinates children with the values basic to a technological society, but this does not invalidate the de-schoolers' case because we certainly do find it advocated as a means of preserving society from overthrow and of producing amenable

workers, intelligent in a limited vocational sphere, but conscious of
the folly of revolting against the laws of economics. What is more,
we find this argument repeatedly advanced at the time when technological society was in the process of development in the early
nineteenth century. Although this tells us little about the purpose of
schooling now, it does suggest a measure of historical justification at
least for the de-schooling view. We can go a little further, for the
organization of education at the turn of the nineteenth and twentieth
centuries was quite explicitly designed to produce adults who would
enter different stations in life, and not only were the curricula of
schools diversified to this end, but also the attitudes and expectations of teachers, even the buildings and amenities. Three different
classes of school were envisaged—public schools, grammar schools,
and elementary schools—producing respectively policy makers,
executives, and operatives, and although intelligence and efficiency
were encouraged at all levels, it was a convergent, limited kind of
intelligence, suitable for making the best of a received policy, but
not for radical innovation. Even at the public school level there was,
in the late nineteenth century, an appreciable tendency for individualism to give way to conformity and consensus.

But at this point doubts begin to emerge. While it is certainly
true that school has often been advocated as a counter-revolutionary
force, it is much less certain that it does in fact help to preserve the
status quo. For every nineteenth-century writer who favoured
education as a means of saving society from upheaval we can quote
another who hoped, or feared, that it would have precisely the
opposite effect. And the evidence gives no support at all to the assertion that education has, in practice, had a stultifying or soporific
effect upon radical criticism. We have seen that one of the prime
purposes of the early nineteenth-century elementary school was to
spread the gospel of the individualist, commercial state. But within
a generation of its victory over paternalism, *laissez-faire* was under
attack, within two it was dying. The attack came from two directions.
The working class developed an alternative philosophy of class
solidarity and mutual support, largely under the influence of
Owenites and Chartists—conspicuous for their prodigious efforts to
achieve education for themselves, and their intense belief in education
as a means of elevating the working classes. Both groups were eager
founders of schools, adult education centres, libraries and discussion
groups. Many of these men received the beginnings of their own

education in public elementary schools. On the other hand were the middle and upper class rebels against *laissez-faire*, all of whom had long institutional education — Coleridge, Carlyle, Maurice, Ruskin, Arnold, Kingsley, Green, and for that matter, Marx. Precisely the same phenomenon occurs at the present time; the de-schoolers refer to it themselves. The really radical social criticism comes from intellectuals, frequently from academics, and one thinks of Marcuse, Roszack, Laing, and notably of Illich, Friere and Goodman. It is the universal experience, historically and geographically, that socialist movements divide into radical wings formed largely of upper and middle class intellectuals, and conservative wings drawing their strength from working men and women. The British Labour movement is an obvious case in point. Students are a conspicuously radical group in all contemporary societies where criticism is permitted, and even in those where totalitarian regimes control the expression of dissentient opinions, they find difficulty in entirely muzzling the universities. Nineteenth-century liberal movements provide a close parallel.

Of course we know that schooling can be used to suppress inconvenient opinions as, for example, in Nazi Germany, and in China and Eastern Europe today. But for this to be effective two conditions must obtain. Teachers must all speak with one voice on all relevant matters, and all other sources of information and discussion must be tightly controlled so that only the official message can get through. Neither of these conditions holds or has held, in this country. The clash between the values of home and school is the subject of agitated comment at the present time. No less obvious are the clashes between school and work, and school and the mass media. Division amongst teachers themselves is acute and chronic, producing for example a plethora of unions with sharply contrasting aims. Some teachers undoubtedly see themselves as guardians of the accepted values of society, but against this we have already noticed that student and pupil power movements have received influential support from dissentient teachers. Under these circumstances, common sense would suggest that education would act rather as an irritant than as a soporific, drawing the attention of at least the more alert and intelligent pupils to the disagreements and tensions underlying apparent consensus, and the history of education since the industrial revolution provides powerful support for the common-sense view.

Finally in this section, an historical study warns us to be cautious of the assertion that drop-out and protest are features peculiar to modern mass education. The truth appears to be exactly the reverse. Hostility towards school by children, and in the lower working class by parents, has been endemic at all periods up to the very late nineteenth century. Few, if any, modern English schools even approach the state of simmering feud, frequently breaking out into open revolt, characteristic of the early nineteenth century public school or board school of the 1870s. What really is new is the appetite for schooling of both pupil and parent, which has been such a powerful factor in causing expansion first of secondary education, and in the 1950s and 1960s of higher education. It is important in the context of the de-schooling controversy to remember that schooling is not something which has been forced upon an unwilling public by an all-powerful establishment, but something which has been granted, rather grudgingly at times, as a result of overwhelming demand. Nothing could illustrate this more clearly than the inability of the Education Department to find a coherent policy for dealing with higher grade schools or, if one seeks a more recent example, the precisely similar incompetence of the Ministry of Education and Department of Education and Science when faced with the explosion of higher education. There is discontent among pupils and students, although its extent is hard to gauge since it is notoriously the discontented who make their views heard; and it is sometimes exacerbated by teachers and administrators. Many schools and colleges have grown too rapidly for their own good, and no one knows yet how to manage really large educational units without leaving gaps in which dissatisfaction may grow and fester. But we may still wish to ask, first whether this is anything new—Shakespeare knew all about it—and second, whether a measure of dissent is not perhaps a healthy sign in a school, indicating that it is in fact education which is being offered, rather than indoctrination.

The function which the de-schoolers think most proper for schools is imparting specific skills and knowledge, and we have seen that one of their basic criticisms of institutional education is that it dilutes instruction by the attention it pays to other functions, especially to custodial care and indoctrination. But they condemn two features of the organization of instruction in schools—compulsory attendance, and sequential syllabuses. They argue for a completely flexible system in which, after perhaps a very basic initial course, pupils and students attend highly specific courses as they see the necessity for them, the task of the administrator merely being to put students into contact with teachers who offer the particular knowledge or skill which they wish to acquire. Perhaps an evening institute is the nearest approach in the English system to the de-schooling model, the provision of courses depending entirely upon public demand, no restriction being placed on combination of courses, and there being no obligation upon anyone to enrol at all or, having enrolled, to attend.

Nineteenth-century experience casts some light on this programme. It suggests, to begin with, that to abolish compulsory schooling would be to increase the advantages of the middle class child, since the evidence is overwhelming that it is children from homes with the least stimulating atmosphere who are most likely to be excluded, and therefore to lose whatever opportunity they might otherwise have had to compensate for their inadequate upbringing. It is not simply a matter of such children lacking knowledge, although this is the case, nor of their being trapped in a restricting linguistic code, although this is also true. Unless the child can be offered a glimpse, if no more, of an alternative way of life to that of their families, they will most likely lack the stimulus to achievement. We are repeatedly told that schools are at fault in providing too many children with experience of failure, thus stunting their development by inhibiting effort, and there is no reason to doubt the truth of this. But the fact is too often ignored that many children bring into school with them cripplingly low levels of aspiration learned at home or from their local community. This is not a new problem resulting from the imposition of an undemocratically selective education system; it was part of the basic data from which nineteenth-century teachers had to work, and it was recognized by contemporaries that perhaps the greatest service of the early board schools was to raise the levels of aspiration of their pupils.

But sheer lack of knowledge may be important, and here again the Victorians learned a lesson which we are in danger of forgetting. Adult education in the nineteenth century was a history of repeated failures to hold the interest of working class students. Mechanics' Institutes, University Extension, the Workers' Educational Association, all started amidst flurries of enthusiasm, with working men signing on eagerly for courses in politics, economics, history and literature in addition to numerous vocational classes. But the upshot was always the same. Working class enrolment fell rapidly away and the courses were taken over by middle class students, only a few highly skilled artisans, foremen etc., remaining from the original clientele. In the case of the Mechanics' Institutes classes frequently failed altogether, and they became recreational centres, useful in themselves but a disappointment to their sponsors. The reason was easy enough to see. Long working hours and depressing living conditions sapped the physical and intellectual stamina of working men, but their great handicap was lack of systematic elementary education, without which they found the courses they were offered simply incomprehensible. As one man remarked about a university extension lecturer: 'I'm all in a fog like—I don't know where I am, and I don't know what he's talking about'. Adult education was attempting to do what the de-schoolers would have us do throughout the educational field, to provide specific courses on demand, without articulation or systematic preparation, and its total failure may give us cause to ponder.

Private schools made the same attempt with the same result. It was their custom to charge fees on a piecemeal basis, the ordinary fee covering only board, if the child was resident and perhaps reading and writing, every other subject being charged separately as extras. The more conscientious proprietors were opposed to this system, recognizing the fairly obvious danger that children would follow totally fragmented courses, their decisions guided by fashion, inertia or sentimental attachments to particular teachers rather than by educational or even vocational considerations. They were, however, quite unable to persuade parents of the virtues of consolidated courses, even where no extra fee was involved. Girls' schools suffered particularly from the system of 'extras', and historians have frequently and correctly commented upon the abysmal triviality of their curricula, in which no subject was explored in enough depth to provide insight or transfer of training, and superficiality was a necessity since every course had to begin from an assumption that the students were entirely ignorant. It is not a heartening precedent, either for abandoning sequential syllabuses, or for the de-schoolers favourite remedy of commercializing educational provision. On the other hand it does suggest that the professional teacher might sometimes know best what constitutes a useful course, leaving aside any consideration of its value as a liberal education, for the pressure for fragmentation and trivialization came from the customer against

R.S.S.—M

the opposition of the teacher. The de-schoolers regard the disestablishment of schools as a necessary step towards a society in which education is a continuous process. In the words of a Unesco report (*Teacher*, 15 September 1972):

> Schools, insofar as they continue to exist as we have known them, cease, under this system, to be reserved to children, and become places of learning for future and present adults. Pupils cease to regard learning as the acquisition of a quantity of knowledge within a certain time; teachers cease to be time-keepers and process chasers and become channels through which pupils can get at the knowledge they need.

It is an inspiring message so long as one does not enquire too closely into its precise meaning, and so long as one does not subscribe to Rousseau's objection to treating children simply as embryo adults. But a historian—and not perhaps a historian alone—may wonder where the evidence is to be found that abolishing formal schooling will produce a great flood of people eager and competent to profit from adult education.

In the introduction I emphasized that this study was only incidentally a critique of de-schooling. The primary aim was to examine the reasons for the emergence of a society in which formal schooling was so prominent a feature that its dismantling could plausibly be suggested as a necessary pre-requisite of social reform. But such an enquiry is not irrelevant to discussion of the de-schoolers case; it can throw light upon their analysis of the situation and upon their recommendations. After all, we do have some experience of what a de-schooled society is like, and of what are the real consequences of mass education. So far, too much of the argument in favour of de-schooling has been at the level of polemical assertion, deriving, it often appears, from pre-conceived political dogma rather than from examination of evidence. Reimer is clearly conscious of this. He writes in his introduction to *School is Dead*: 'I do not expect to satisfy the norms of academic scholarship. To do that I would have to write not this book now, but a completely different book twenty years from now.' One can sympathize, but the danger is not so much of failing to satisfy academic norms, but of removing the topic entirely from the realms of rational discussion. When he writes, for example, on the same page, 'When techniques, institutions and ideologies were primitive, man lived in relative equality and freedom, because there were no adequate means of domination,' it is, I think not merely an academic historian who longs to hear the comments of Wat Tyler or one of the victims of Attila or Genghiz Khan. And when a speaker at the annual conference of college of education students remarks (*Times Educational Supplement*, 22 September 1972) that: 'All teachers are conservative, they are bureaucrats paid to conserve society, not challenge it', it is not merely carping to ask whether there really are no radical teachers at all; what, except for a useful term of generalized abuse, are we to make of the word 'bureaucrat' in this context; what kind of conduct the speaker would allow to be 'challenge' to society; who decreed that teachers could not make this challenge, and where the decree is recorded. The controversy is seriously in need of deflation by an injection of verifiable material, so that it may proceed at the level of rational argument and counter-argument, rather than by the confrontation of rival confessions of faith. It has been my aim in this historical study to contribute to this end.

Bibliography

Adamson, J. W. (1930) *English Education 1789-1902*, Cambridge University Press.

Altick, R. D. (1957) *The English Common Reader*, Chicago University Press.

Argles, M. (1964) *South Kensington to Robbins*, Longmans.

Armytage, W. H. G. (1965) *The Rise of the Technocrats*, Routledge & Kegan Paul.

Ashworth, W. (1960) *An Economic History of England, 1870-1939*, Methuen.

Bamford, T. W. (1965) *The Evolution of Rural Education, 1850-1964*, Hull University Press.

Bamford, T. W. (1967) *The Rise of the Public Schools*, Nelson.

Banks, O. (1955) *Parity and Prestige in English Secondary Education*, Routledge & Kegan Paul.

Barnard, H. C. (1961) *A History of English Education from 1760*, University of London Press, 2nd ed., 1961.

Barraclough, G. (1967) *An Introduction to Contemporary History*, Penguin Books.

Bell, Q. (1963) *The Schools of Design*, Routledge & Kegan Paul.

Bernbaum, G. (1967) *Social Change and the Schools, 1918-1944*, Routledge & Kegan Paul.

Bishop, A. S. (1971) *The Rise of a Central Authority for English Education*, Cambridge University Press.

Boyd, W., and Rawson, W. (1965) *The Story of the New Education*, Heinemann.

Briggs, A. (1959) *The Age of Improvement*, Longmans.

Briggs, A. (ed.) (1962) *Chartist Studies*, Macmillan.

Briggs, A. (1963) *Victorian Cities*, Odhams.

Briggs, A. (1965) *Victorian People*, Penguin Books.

Briggs, A., and Saville, J. (1967) *Essays in Labour History*, Macmillan.

Bruce, M. (1965) *The Coming of the Welfare State*, Batsford, 2nd ed.

Bullock, A., and Shock, M. (1956) *The Liberal Tradition*, Black.

Burgess, H. J. (1958) *Enterprise in Education*, SPCK.

Burns, T., and Saul, S. B. (1967) *Social Theory and Economic Change*, Tavistock.

Burrow, J. W. (1966) *Evolution and Society*, Cambridge University Press.

Burston, W. H. (1969) *James Mill on Education*, Cambridge University Press.

Central Advisory Council for Education (England) (1959) Crowther Report, *Fifteen to Eighteen*, HMSO.

Chaloner, W. H. (1950) *The Social and Economic Development of Crewe, 1780-1923*, Manchester University Press.

Checkland, S. G. (1964) *The Rise of Industrial Society in England, 1815-1885*, Longmans.

Clark, G. Kitson (1962) *The Making of Victorian England*, Metheun.

Clark, G. Kitson (1967) *An Expanding Society*, Cambridge University Press.

Clarke, F. (1940) *Education and Social Change*, Sheldon Press.

Claxton, T. (1844) *Hints to Mechanics on Self Education and Mutual Instruction*, London.

Collins, P. (1963) *Dickens and Education*, Macmillan.

Consultative Committee upon Secondary Education (1938) *Spens Report.*

Cotgrove, S. F. (1958) *Technical Education and Social Change*, Allen & Unwin.

Coveney, P. (1967) *The Image of Childhood*, Penguin Books.

Cruikshank, M. (1964) *Church and State in English Education*, Macmillan.

Committee of Privy Council for Scientific and Industrial Research (1916) P.P., Vol. VIII.

Dobbs, A. E. (1919) *Education and Social Movements 1700-1850*, Longman.

Eager, E. McG. (1953) *Making Men*, London University Press.

Eaglesham, E. J. R. (1967) *The Foundations of Twentieth Century Education in England*, Routledge & Kegan Paul.

Ensor, R. C. K. (1936) *England, 1870-1914*, Oxford University Press.

Entwhistle, H. (1971) *Child-centred Education*, Methuen.

Evans, E. G. S. (1971) *Modern Educational Psychology*, Routledge & Kegan Paul.

Friere, P. (1972) *Pedagogy of the Oppressed*, Sheed & Ward.

Furth, C. (1966) *Life Since 1900*, Allen & Unwin, 3rd ed.

Goodman, P. (1971) *Compulsory Mis-education*, Penguin Books.

Goodman, P. (1970) *Growing-up Absurd*, Sphere.

Graves, J. (1943) *Policy and Progress in Secondary Education 1902-1942*, Nelson.

Graves, R., and Hodge, A. (1950) *The Long Week-end*, Faber.

Gregg, P. (1967) *The Welfare State*, Harrap.

Guttsman, W. L. (1965) *The British Political Elite*, MacGibbon & Kee.

Haldane, R. B. (1902) *Education and Empire*, Murray.

Halsey, A. H., Floud, J., and Anderson, C. A. (1961) *Education, Economy and Society*, Collier-Macmillan.

Hamburger, J. (1965) *Intellectuals in Politics*, Yale University Press.

Hans, N. (1951) *New Trends in Education in the Eighteenth Century*, Routledge & Kegan Paul.

Harrison, J. F. C. (1961) *Learning and Living, 1790-1960*, Routledge & Kegan Paul.

Hayes, C. J. H. (1963) *A Generation of Materialism*, Harper.

Heeney, B. (1969) *Mission to the Middle Classes*, SPCK.

Himmelfarb, G. (1968) *Victorian Minds*, Weidenfeld & Nicolson.

History of Education Society (1970) *Studies in the Government and Control of Education since 1860*, Methuen.

Hobsbawm, E. J. (1968) *Industry and Empire*, Weidenfeld & Nicolson.

Holmes, E. (1911) *What is, and What Might Be*, Constable.

Holt, J. (1968) *How Children Learn*, Pitman.

Holt, J. (1969) *How Children Fail*, Penguin Books.

Holt, J. (1970) *Understanding Schools*, Pitman.

Holt, J. (1971) *The Underachieving School*, Penguin Books.

Houghton, W. E. (1957) *The Victorian Frame of Mind*, Yale University Press.

Hughes, H. S. (1959) *Consciousness and Society*, MacGibbon & Kee.

Hughes, R. E. (1901) *Schools at Home and Abroad*, Sonnenschein.

Hutchins, R. M. (1970) *The Learning Society*, Penguin Books.

Hutchinson, M., and Young, C. (1962) *Educating the Intelligent*, Penguin Books.

Illich, I. D. (1971) *De-schooling Society*, Calder & Boyars.

Inglis, K. S. (1963) *Churches and the Working Class in Victorian England*, Routledge & Kegan Paul.

Jackson, H. (1913) *The Eighteen Nineties*, Grant Richards.

Jaeger, M. (1956) *Before Victoria*, Chatto & Windus.

Jones, M. G. (1964) *The Charity School Movement*, Cass.

Judges, A. V. (1952) *Pioneers of English Education*, Faber.

Kay-Shuttleworth, J. P. (1969) *Memorandum on Popular Education* (first published 1868, reprinted by Woburn Press, 1969).

Kazamias, A. M. (1966) *Politics, Society and Secondary Education in England*, Pennsylvania University Press.

Kornhauser, W. (1960) *The Politics of Mass Society*, Routledge & Kegan Paul.

Leavis, F. R. (ed.) (1950) *Mill on Bentham and Coleridge*, Chatto & Windus.

Lester-Smith, W. O. (1965) *The Government of Education*, Penguin Books.

Lowndes, G. A. N. (1969) *The Silent Social Revolution*, Oxford University Press, 2nd ed.

McClelland, D. C. (1961) *The Achieving Society*, Van Nostrand.

Maccoby, S. (1935) *English Radicalism 1832-1852*, Allen & Unwin.

Mack, E. C. (1938) *Public Schools and British Opinion, 1780-1860*, Methuen.

Mack, E. C. (1941) *Public Schools and British Opinion Since 1860*, Columbia University Press.

McLeish, J. (1969) *Evangelical Religion and Popular Education*, Methuen.

McLeish, J. (1969) *The Theory of Social Change*, Routledge & Kegan Paul.

Maclure, J. S. (1970) *One Hundred Years of London Education*, Allen Lane.

Malthus, T. R. (1798) *Essay on the Principle of Population*.

Marsh, D. C. (1965) *The Changing Social Structure of England and Wales, 1871-1961*, Routledge & Kegan Paul, 2nd ed.

Marwick, A. (1970) *Britain in the Century of Total War*, Penguin Books.

Mather, F. C. (1959) *Public Order in the Age of the Chartists*, Manchester University Press.

Mathews, H. F. (1945) *Methodism and the Education of the People*, Epworth.

Minutes of the Committee of Council on Education, vol. I (1845), 2 vols, Parker & Son.

Montgomery, R. J. (1965) *Examinations*, Longmans.

Mowat, C. L. (1955) *Britain Between the Wars*, Methuen.

Murphy, J. (1971) *Church, State and Schools in Britain, 1800-1970*, Routledge & Kegan Paul.

Musgrave, P. W. (1968) *Society and Education in England Since 1800*, Methuen.

Musgrave, P. W. (1970) *Sociology, History and Education*, Methuen.

Musgrove, F. (1964) *Youth and the Social Order*, Routledge & Kegan Paul.

Musgrove, F. (1966) *The Family, Education and Society*, Routledge & Kegan Paul.

Musgrove, F. (1971) *Patterns of Power and Authority in English Education*, Methuen.

Musgrove, F., and Taylor, P. H. (1969) *Society and the Teacher's Role*, Routledge & Kegan Paul.

National Union of Teachers, *Investment for National Survival*, n.d.(c. 1962).

Newsome, D. (1961) *Godliness and Good Learning*, Murray.

Owen, D. (1965) *English Philanthropy*, Oxford University Press.

Paine, Thomas (1792) *The Rights of Man*.

Pelling, H. (1960) *Modern Britain, 1885-1955*, Nelson.

Pelling, H. (1965) *The Origins of the Labour Party 1880-1900*, Oxford University Press, 2nd ed.

Perkin, H. (1969) *The Origins of Modern English Society*, Routledge & Kegan Paul.

Peterson, A. D. C. (1960) *A Hundred Years of Education*, Duckworth, 2nd. ed.

Pinchbeck, I., and Hewitt, M. (1970) *Children in English Society*, vol. I, Routledge & Kegan Paul.

Poynter, J. R. (1969) *Society and Pauperism*, Routledge & Kegan Paul.

Reimer, E. (1971) *School is Dead*, Penguin Books.

Rich, R. W. (1933) *The Training of Teachers*, Cambridge University Press.

Richter, M. (1964) *The Politics of Conscience*, Weidenfeld & Nicolson.

Robbins Committee (1963) *Higher Education*, HMSO.

Roberts, D. (1960) *Victorian Origins of the British Welfare State*, Yale University Press.

Rostow, W. W. (1948) *British Economy of the Nineteenth Century*, Oxford University Press.

Rostow, W. W. (1960) *The Stages of Economic Growth*, Cambridge University Press.

Roszak, T. (1968) *The Making of a Counter Culture*, Faber.

Rubinstein, D., and Simon, B. (1969) *The Evolution of the Comprehensive School 1926-1966*, Routledge & Kegan Paul.

Saville, J. (1954) *Democracy and the Labour Movement*, Lawrence & Wishart.

Schenk, H. G. (1966) *The Mind of the European Romantics*, Constable.

Selleck, R. J. W. (1968) *The New Education*, Pitman.

Selleck, R. J. W. (1972) *English Primary Education and the Progressives*, Routledge & Kegan Paul.

Semmel, B. (1960) *Imperialism and Social Reform*, Allen & Unwin.

Senior, N. (1861) *Suggestion on Popular Education*.

Shipman, M. (1971) *Education and Modernization*, Faber.

Silver, H. (1965) *The Concept of Popular Education*, MacGibbon & Kee.

Silver, H. (1969) *Robert Owen on Education*, Cambridge University Press.

Simon, B. (1960) *Studies in the History of Education 1780-1870*, Lawrence & Wishart.

Simon, B. (1965) *Education and the Labour Movement, 1870-1920*, Lawrence & Wishart.

Smith, F. (1923) *The Life and Work of Sir James Kay-Shuttleworth*, Murray.

Smith, F. (1931) *A History of English Elementary Education, 1760-1902*, London University Press.

Smith, F. B. (1966) *The Making of the Second Reform Bill*, Cambridge University Press.

Smith, P., and Summerfield, G. (1969) *Matthew Arnold and the Education of the New Order*, Cambridge University Press.

Tawney, R. H. (1964) *Equality*, Allen & Unwin, 4th ed.

Thompson, E. P. (1963) *The Making of the English Working Class*, Gollancz.

Thomson, D. (1950) *England in the Nineteenth Century*, Penguin Books.

Thomson, D. (1965) *England in the Twentieth Century*, Penguin Books.

Tobias, J. J. (1967) *Crime and Industrial Society in the Nineteenth Century*, Batsford.

Tropp, A. (1957) *The School Teachers*, Heinemann.

Vaizey, J. (1962) *The Economics of Education*, Faber.

Vaughan, M., and Scotford Archer, M. (1972) *Social Conflict and Educational Change in England and France, 1789-1848*, Cambridge University Press.

Wardle, D. (1970) *English Popular Education, 1780-1970*, Cambridge University Press.

Wardle, D. (1971) *Education and Society in Nineteenth Century Nottingham*, Cambridge University Press.

Wearmouth, R. F. (1948) *Some Working Class Movements of the Nineteenth Century*, Epworth.

Webb, R. K. (1955) *The British Working Class Reader, 1790-1848*, Allen & Unwin.

Webb, S. (1901) article in *Nineteenth Century and After*, no. 295.

Webb, S. (1904) *London Education*, Longmans.

Wells, A. (1847) *On the Education of the Working Class*, London.

West, E. G. (1965) *Education and the State*, Institute of Economic Affairs.

Williams, C. H. (1967) *English Historical Documents, 1485-1558*, Eyre & Spottiswoode.

Williams, R. (1951) *Culture and Society, 1780-1950*, Penguin Books.

Wood, A. C. (1953) *History of University College, Nottingham*, Blackwell.

Young, G. M. (1953) *Victorian England: Portrait of an Age*, Oxford University Press, 2nd ed.

Young, G. M. (1962) *Victorian Essays*, Oxford University Press.

Young, M. (1961) *The Rise of the Meritocracy*, Penguin Books.

Index